The Freedom of Religious Expression
in Public Universities and High Schools

JOHN W. WHITEHEAD

The Freedom of Religious Expression in Public Universities and High Schools

THE RUTHERFORD INSTITUTE REPORT: VOLUME 1

Second Edition

CROSSWAY BOOKS • WESTCHESTER, ILLINOIS
A DIVISION OF GOOD NEWS PUBLISHERS

First printing, 1983
Second printing, 1984
First printing, second edition, 1986

Printed in the United States of America

Library of Congress Catalog Card Number 83-72040

ISBN 0-89107-295-0

Contents

Acknowledgments

As with anything, there are those whose assistance makes a project a better project. Such was true with this book.

I would like to express my gratitude to Franky Schaeffer for his encouragement on this book.

The comments and suggestions of Tom Neuberger and Jim Knicely were valuable. David Myers' research and Richard Moore's work on the footnotes is also appreciated. Kimberly Britts', Ken Clark's, and John Pyle's work in the final stages of this edition was valuable. Rebecca Beane's proofreading of the galleys was also valuable.

Finally, I am in great sympathy with all those who have struggled to maintain freedom of religious expression in the universities and public schools. Without you, such expression would be much more limited.

The Freedom of Religious Expression in Public Universities and High Schools

Preface

There has been some confusion surrounding the rights of religious persons to express themselves in the universities and public schools. In the following pages I will discuss this important subject in both the historical and modern perspectives. The historical perspective, often ignored, suggests that our forefathers would have permitted much more latitude toward religious expression than is commonly found in our modern secular society.

When discussing the rights of religious persons, it must not be forgotten that at stake are the rights and freedoms of students, faculty members, administrators, and non-students. As might be expected, a considerable number of cases have upheld the rights of students and faculty members to express themselves, with some limitations, in the context of the state university and public education system.

In recent years the controversy over religious expression in public education has been heightened by the rise of the recognition of student and teacher rights. Some believe that any mention of religion in public education classrooms is against the law.

The United States Supreme Court, in its role of

interpreting the Constitution, has not taken this position in its decisions. To the contrary, the Court has held that the government (which includes the public schools) must accommodate religion whenever it is constitutionally required. The Court has expressly held that religious speech enjoys the same high First Amendment protection as other speech under the freedom of speech clause in addition to its First Amendment protection under the freedom of religious exercise clause. Moreover, through the passage of the Equal Access Act, Congress has expressed its view that religious free speech must be treated fairly and equally within the public schools.

Therefore, this book emphasizes that the American system was intended to operate on the principles of free and open communication. When and if free communication is stifled, the system suffers and, along with it, the cause of freedom.

1

A Historical Perspective

[A]ll freedoms hang together. . . . Civil liberties scarcely thrive when religious liberties are disregarded, and the reverse is equally true. Beneath them all is a philosophy of liberty which assumes a measure of variety in human behavior, honors integrity, respects the dignity of man, and seeks to exemplify the compassion of God.

Historian Roland Bainton

The Northwest Ordinance of 1787, which set aside federal property in the territory for schools and which was passed again by Congress in 1789 (the same Congress that drafted the Constitution), states:

Religion, morality, and knowledge being necessary to good government and the happiness of mankind, schools and the means of learning shall forever be encouraged.

From this foundation our nation's schools were born. Part of that foundation—according to the Northwest Ordinance—was religion.

In looking at the historical record, one sees that religion was integrated into the public school curriculum. Textbooks referred to God without embarrassment, and public schools considered one of their major tasks to be the development of character through the teaching of religion. For example, the *New England Primer* opened with certain religious admonitions followed by the Lord's Prayer, the Apostles' Creed, the Ten Commandments, and the names of the books of the Bible.

The influence of William Holmes McGuffey, a philosopher and a professor at the University of Virginia, was remarkable. His *Eclectic Readers* were published in 1836, and from that year until 1920—two years after Mississippi became the last state to institute a public school system—his books sold more than 120 million copies, a total that put them in a class with only the Bible and *Webster's Dictionary*.[1] McGuffey's *Readers* stressed, as did the Northwest Ordinance, "religion, morality, and knowledge," in that order. Historian Henry Steele Commager, in an introduction for a reissue of *McGuffey's Fifth Reader*, writes:

> What was the nature of the morality that permeated the *Readers*? It was deeply religious, and . . . religion then meant a Protestant Christianity. . . . The world of the *McGuffeys* was a world where no one questioned the truths of the Bible or their relevance to everyday contact. . . . The *Readers*, therefore, are filled with stories from the Bible, and tributes to its truth and beauty.[2]

The great men who built this country from the ground up sat under McGuffey-type teaching. This type of teaching produced a spirit of accommodation toward the exercise of religion in early America. This is especially apparent in the men who drafted the Constitution.

For example, one of the earliest acts of the first House of Representatives was to elect a chaplain. On May 1, 1789, the House elected as chaplain the Reverend William Linn. Five hundred dollars was appropriated from the federal treasury to pay his salary.[3] Recently a legislator in Nebraska challenged the constitutionality of the Nebraska legislature's practice of beginning each of its sessions with a prayer by a state-paid chaplain. The United States Supreme Court, relying on the actions of the first House of Representatives, found the practice to be constitutional.[4]

Congress proposed a joint resolution on September 24, 1789, which was intended to allow the people of the United States an opportunity to thank God for affording them an opportunity to establish this country.[5] This proclamation was submitted to President George Washington the very day after Congress had voted to recommend to the states the final text of what has become the First Amendment to the United States Constitution.[6] As President, James Madison likewise issued four prayer proclamations.[7]

While Thomas Jefferson undoubtedly believed that church and state should be separate, his actions in public life demonstrate that he did not espouse the absolute separation advocated by some modern proponents of separation of church and state. For example, on October 31, 1803, President Jefferson proposed to the United States Senate a treaty with the Kaskaskian Indians. This treaty provided that federal money be used to support a Catholic priest and to build a church (a Catholic mission) for the ministry of the Kaskaskian Indians. The treaty was ratified by Congress on December 23, 1803.[8]

When Congress initially authorized the public schools for the nation's capital, the first president of the Washington, D.C. school board was Thomas Jefferson himself.[9] In fact, he "was the chief author of the first plan of public education adopted for the city of Washington."[10] The first official report on file indicates that the Bible and the *Watts Hymnal* were the principal, if not the only, books then in use for reading by the Washington, D.C. public school student.[11]

As one can readily see, history clearly teaches[12] that from our country's inception the prevailing mood toward religion has been one of accommodation. The founding fathers and those who administered and taught in the public schools throughout the nineteenth century defended and perpetuated this accommodation.

Without this view, the freedom of expression of those in the religious minority is severely restricted. As James Madison once told Congress, the Bill of Rights points "sometimes against the abuse of executive power, sometimes against the legislative, and, in some cases, against the community itself; or, in other words, against the majority in favor of the minority."[13]

2

Accommodating Neutrality

Congress shall make no law respecting an establishment of religion, or prohibiting the free exercise thereof; or abridging the freedom of speech, or of the press; or the right of the people peaceably to assemble, and to petition the Government for a redress of grievances.

The First Amendment

The First Amendment dictates that (1) the state may not establish one religion over others, and (2) the state must allow for the freedom to exercise one's religion. As interpreted by the United States Supreme Court, this essentially means the state must remain neutral in matters of religion so that it does not prefer one religion over other religions or exhibit hostility toward one or all religions or any particular religion.

Accommodating Neutrality
Instead of taking a position of strict neutrality (the absolute separation of religion and state), the United States Supreme Court has taken the approach of "ac-

commodating neutrality." This position holds that the First Amendment was intended to maintain a proper relationship between the government and religion. Thus, although there may be a "wall of separation" between church and state, it is not an impregnable wall. As a consequence, not all relationships between government and religion are unconstitutional. In other words, the state must accommodate or aid religion in certain circumstances.

As such, *accommodation* of religion is *mandated.* The Supreme Court made this clear in 1984 in *Lynch v. Donnelly*[1] There the Court held:

> [T]he Constitution [does not] require complete separation of church and state; *it affirmatively mandates accommodation,* not mere tolerance, of all religions, and forbids hostility toward any. . . . Anything less would require the "callous indifference" we have said was never intended by the Establishment Clause. . . . Indeed, we have observed such hostility would bring us into "war with our national tradition as embodied in the First Amendment's guaranty of the free exercise of religion."[2]

Recently, however, the Supreme Court has stressed the need for a more reserved accommodation of religion. In *Wallace v. Jaffree,*[3] the Court held that Alabama's allowance of a period of silence for meditation or voluntary prayer in public schools violated the Establishment Clause. Although the Court restricted the neutrality concept, the decisive factor in the Court's analysis was the avowed legislative intent underlying the statute. The statute's effect was meant to revive "voluntary prayer . . . as a step in the right direction."[4] Based on the state's sectarian intent, the Court could reasonably foresee attempts to advance religion, not merely to accommodate it. Therefore, the Court was faced with facts requiring an aberrational decision on accommodating neutrality in public schools.

The accommodation of religion by the state is, then, the essence of the Supreme Court's position of neutrality toward religion. State indifference toward religion, however, does not conform to the Court's definition of neutrality. Instead, a disinterested insensibility exhibited by the state toward religion is a subtle form of hostility. In respect to such state indifference to the religious element in our society, former Supreme Court Justice William O. Douglas remarked:

> That would be preferring those who believe in no religion over those who do believe. . . . But we find no constitutional requirement which makes it necessary for government to be hostile to religion and to throw its weight against efforts to widen the effective scope of religious influence.[5]

The accommodating neutrality approach (or what can be referred to as "mandated accommodation") has been expressed by the Supreme Court in numerous decisions.[6] For example, in the *Walz v. Tax Commission*[7] decision, Supreme Court Chief Justice Burger spoke of a *"benevolent neutrality* which will permit religious exercise to exist without sponsorship and without interference."[8]

Concerning the supposed separation of church and state, Justice Blackmun in the 1976 case of *Roemer v. Board of Public Works of Maryland*[9] remarked that the "Court has enforced a scrupulous neutrality by the State, as among religions and also as between religious and other activities, but *a hermetic separation of the two is an impossibility it has never required.*"[10]

In the context of accommodating neutrality, the United States Supreme Court has formulated a tripartite test to determine whether or not the First Amendment establishment of religion prohibition has been transgressed. The test, as stated by the Court, is as follows:

> First, the statute must have a secular legislative purpose; second, its *principal* or *primary* effect must be one that neither advances nor inhibits religion; finally, the statute must not foster "an *excessive* government entanglement with religion."[11]

Keeping in mind the Supreme Court's position on accommodation of religion, it is little wonder that the key phrases in the tripartite test are "principal or primary effect" and "excessive entanglement." Therefore, in applying the test to a particular religious practice, if that practice no more than "incidentally" benefits religion, it passes the Supreme Court's muster. As Justice Blackmun stated in the *Roemer* decision:

Everson and *Allen* put to rest any argument that the State may never act in such a way that has the *incidental effect of facilitating religious activity.* . . . If this were impermissible . . . a church could not be protected by the police and fire department, or have its public sidewalk kept in repair. The Court never has held that religious activities must be discriminated against in this way.[12]

To be specific, the Supreme Court has designated only five particular practices as unconstitutional establishments of religion in the public schools. These are:

(1) State-directed and required on-premises religious training, in *McCollum v. Board of Education;*[13]

(2) State-directed and required prayer, in *Engel v. Vitale;*[14]

(3) State-directed and required Bible reading, in *School District of Abington Townships, Pa. v. Schempp;*[15]

(4) State-directed and required posting of the Ten Commandments, in *Stone v. Graham.*[16]

(5) State-directed and authorized "period of silence" for meditation and voluntary prayer, in *Wallace v. Jaffree.*[17]

In these five fact situations the government sponsored and was actively involved in the particular religious activity.

Unfortunately, many school administrations have misinterpreted the various Supreme Court cases as deciding that any religious expression is unconstitutional on the public school campus. It was such oversweeping interpretations of United States Supreme Court decisions which caused Justice Clark, author of the *Schempp* decision, to remark: "Most commentators suggested that the court had outlawed religious observances in public schools when, in fact, the court did nothing of the kind."[18]

In fact, the Supreme Court in the *Schempp* case stressed that religion can be taught within the public schools if it is taught *objectively*.[19] Justice William Brennan in his concurring opinion in *Schempp* explained what it means to teach religion "objectively" when he stated that "teaching *about* the Holy Scriptures" does not run afoul of the Constitution.[20]

The Court's emphasis has been on *communication* versus indoctrination in the public school system. What is the difference? Indoctrination offers no option or alternative point of view. Communication is a transfer of information.

Again, the Supreme Court has warned that what may appear to be an indifferent neutrality in some instances may actually be a form of impermissible hostility toward religion. Justice Arthur Goldberg, concurring in the Bible-reading decision in *Schempp*, noted:

[U]ntutored devotion to the concept of neutrality can
lead to invocation or approval of results which partake
not simply of that noninterference and noninvolvement
with the religious which the Constitution commands,
but of a brooding and pervasive devotion to the secular
and a passive, or even active, hostility to the religious.
Such results are not only not compelled by the Constitution, but, it seems to me, are prohibited by it.[21]

In avoidance of such subtle hostility, the Supreme
Court has assumed the position of accommodating neutrality. Justice William O. Douglas even predicted the
result if accommodating neutrality were not the position of the Supreme Court:

Prayers in our legislative halls; the appeals to the Almighty in the messages of the Chief Executive; the
proclamations making Thanksgiving Day a holiday; "so
help me God" in our courtroom oaths—these and all
other references to the Almighty that run through our
laws, our public rituals, our ceremonies would be flout-
ing the First Amendment. A fastidious atheist or agnos-
tic could even object to the supplication with which the
Court opens each session: "God save the United States
and this Honorable Court."[22]

It is emphasized that in *Engel, Schempp,* and other
cases the Supreme Court has not abandoned the doctrine of accommodating neutrality. To the contrary, by
rejecting such practices as mandatory prayer and Bible
reading in the public schools, the Supreme Court was
merely defining some of the limits of the doctrine.

The Religion of Secularism

The Court has also recognized the possibility of hostility toward religion in the context of secularistic trends of modern society. In this respect, Justice Tom Clark, speaking for the Supreme Court, observed in *Schempp* that "the State may not establish a 'religion of secularism' in the sense of affirmatively opposing or showing hostility to religion, thus 'preferring those who believe in no religion over those who do believe.' "[23]

The prohibition against establishing a religion of secularism was strengthened in *Torcaso v. Watkins,*[24] where the Supreme Court recognized that the First Amendment grants the same protection to and imposes the same limitations on secular or humanistic religions as are applicable to theistic religions.[25] It logically follows, then, that the government is prohibited from establishing nontheistic or secular ideologies in the public schools, just as it is prohibited from establishing theistic practices. As one legal commentator has written:

> [I]f the total impact of a school value program is to promote a humanistic ideology, or if it utilizes the practices of a humanistic religion, it may be held that the state is aiding and preferring a secular religion.[26]

A "religion of secularism" may be established by school authorities when they deny religious expression to students and teachers either within the classroom or elsewhere on campus. This would be "preferring those who believe in no religion over those who do believe" in religion.[27]

To avoid establishing a religion of secularism, school authorities must accommodate students who desire to express their religion. Moreover, school authorities should cooperate with faculty members' and students' attempts to make their classrooms and student organizations available to off-campus speakers who may speak on a topic of religious content or who may present a secular subject from a religious viewpoint.

Not only does this type of cooperation on the part of school officials permissibly accommodate the religious needs of its faculty and students, but it also avoids those acts hostile to religion and thus contrary to the Constitution. As Justice Douglas said so well:

> When the state encourages religious instruction or cooperates with religious authorities by adjusting the schedule of public events to sectarian needs, it follows the best of our traditions. For it then respects the religious nature of our people and accommodates the public service to their spiritual needs.[28]

3
The Rights of Students

All ideas having even the slightest redeeming social importance—unorthodox ideas, controversial ideas, even ideas hateful to the prevailing climate of opinion—have the full protection of the [First Amendment].

Roth v. United States, 354 U.S. 476, 484 (1957)

There was a time in American history when doubt existed as to whether minors and, in particular, secondary school students are protected by the guarantees of the United States Constitution. That doubt has now been removed.

In many varied contexts, the Supreme Court and numerous lesser tribunals have declared that minors have constitutional rights comparable to those of adults. For example, the Court, in considering the rights of juvenile criminal offenders, held that the Constitution is not for adults alone.[1]

Although juvenile rights have been the subject of much litigation in the area of criminal law, the most

27

litigious area with regard to minors' rights has been in the context of education and the public school community. Not surprisingly, the rights of minor students have been broadened and have become more firmly entrenched as a result of court litigation in this area.

The Tinker Test

Any discussion concerning the First Amendment rights available to students must begin with the landmark case of *Tinker v. Des Moines Independent Community School District.*[2] The issue in *Tinker* was whether the wearing of armbands by public high school students during school hours in protest of the Vietnam war was constitutionally protected under the First Amendment.

The Supreme Court held that the wearing of the armbands was a form of free expression so closely akin to "pure speech" as to be "entitled to comprehensive protection under the First Amendment."[3] The Court emphasized that in "the absence of a specific showing of constitutionally valid reasons to regulate their speech, students are entitled to freedom of expression of their views."[4]

In an attempt to define what would constitute "constitutionally valid reasons" to regulate free expression, the Supreme Court in *Tinker* formulated a two-pronged test. A student's freedom of expression is guaranteed on the public high school campus if it does not:

(1) *materially* and *substantially* interfere with the requirements of appropriate discipline in the operation of the school; and,

(2) does not *invade* or *collide* with the rights of others.[5]

If student expression meets these two requirements, then any interference with such student expression on the part of school officials is constitutionally suspect.

The *Tinker* rationale was recently followed in an important case. In *Widmar v. Vincent*[6] the United States Supreme Court upheld the right of a student religious group to meet on the campus of the University of Missouri at Kansas City. The University of Missouri had prohibited the use of its buildings or grounds "for purposes of religious worship or religious teaching,"[7] saying that permitting use for religious purposes would violate separation of church and state. This regulation, the Supreme Court held, was contrary to the guarantees of free speech and free association under the First Amendment.[8]

In line with *Tinker*, the Court recognized "a university's right to exclude even First Amendment activities that violate reasonable campus rules or substantially interfere with the opportunity of other students to obtain an education."[9] This, however, was the only permissible limitation on First Amendment activities.

In applying the *Tinker* test to the right of students to freedom of expression, religious or otherwise, the Supreme Court's insistence that a "student's rights . . .

do not embrace merely the classroom hours"[10] should be kept in mind. Moreover, given the *Tinker* holding and its subsequent affirmation in later decisions, the right to the freedom of religious expression must be protected by public school authorities to the same extent as freedom of nonreligious expression. This is true unless it can be shown that such expression would materially and substantially interfere with appropriate school discipline or that it would collide with or invade the rights of others.

Prior Restraints on Free Speech

Any ban on free expression by students must also be analyzed in light of the Supreme Court's stand against any prior restraints on free speech. A prior restraint on free speech occurs when state officials attempt to or do in fact suppress speech *before* it is uttered. As one legal commentator has remarked, "It is quite clear that the Court has chosen to react strongly against any prior-inform governmental encroachment on free expression."[11]

In *Tinker* the Supreme Court held that prior restraints on student expression would be permissible only in the presence of "*facts* which might reasonably have led school authorities to *forecast substantial disruption of* or material interference with school activities."[12] The Court's core word "facts" is essential to an understanding of the Court's statement[13] because the Court has previously refused to sanction prior restraints merely on the basis of past experience.[14] The same limitations exist for prior restraints on religious exercise as for prior restraints on speech.

In the context of religious expression, a prior restraint would be justified only if the *facts* of the situation supported a *reasonable* belief on the part of school officials that such expression would cause substantial and material disruption or interference with school discipline. The Supreme Court in *Tinker* distinguished such a reasonable belief from an "undifferentiated fear or apprehension of disturbance [which] is not enough to overcome the right to freedom of expression" in high schools.[15] As one legal commentator has said, *Tinker*, "despite permitting some restraints, grants extensive first amendment rights to high school students, rights not subject to limitations merely to prevent embarrassment or discomfiture to school authorities."[16]

Gay Students Organization of the University of New Hampshire v. Bonner[17] is a case of importance which relies on the reasoning of *Tinker.* A federal court of appeals affirmed a lower court decision granting a gay student organization the right to meet on a state university campus. An ongoing program of student organizations existed at the state university, but university officials denied the gay group permission to hold social functions on campus.

The court in *Gay Students* insisted: "It is well established that 'above all else, the First Amendment means that government has no power to restrict expression because of its message, its ideas, its subject matter, or its content.' "[18] The court emphasized that the "fact that the GSO [Gay Student Organization] *alone* was made subject to the regulation indicates that the ban is *content-related*."[19]

A ban on certain types of religious expression on the university campus or in the public high school generally indicates that such restrictions are *content-related*. The Supreme Court in *Tinker* addressed this specific point: "Clearly, the prohibition of expression of *one particular* opinion, at least without evidence that it is necessary to avoid material and substantial interference with school work or discipline, is not constitutionally permissible."[20]

Freedom of Association

Over twenty years ago the Supreme Court stated that "[i]t is beyond debate that freedom to engage in association for the advancement of beliefs and ideas is an inseparable aspect of the 'liberty' assured by the Due Process Clause of the Fourteenth Amendment which embraces freedom of speech."[21] What was originally called the freedom of assembly, but is now often referred to as the freedom of association, has in recent years been extended to students.

In *Healy v. James*[22] the Court held unanimously that any limitation or denial of the freedom of speech or association by a state on the basis of a subject matter which is neither slanderous nor obscene is violative of students' First Amendment rights. *Healy* concerned a group of student activists, the Students for a Democratic Society, which sought and was denied recognition as a student organization at a Connecticut state college.

Justice William Powell, writing for the Court, recognized an inherent general freedom of association within the First Amendment and explained that colleges and universities are not immune to the amendment's sweep.[23] The Supreme Court held the college's denial of recognition to be a prior restraint on the First Amendment freedom of association. Although this particular decision involved students at a state university, the same rule should apply at the public high school level as well.[24]

Tinker is also relevant in determining the extent to which a high school student's freedom of association comes within the scope of constitutional protection. The Court in *Tinker* specifically stated that the "principal use to which the schools are dedicated is to accommodate students during prescribed hours for the purpose of certain types of activities. Among those activities is *personal intercommunication* among the students."[25] In fact, in the *Gay Students* decision, the court held that students have a right to freedom of association, and "it is immaterial whether the beliefs sought to be advanced by associations pertain to political, economic, *religious* or cultural matters."[26]

The Right to Receive Information: The "Right to Hear"

Pertinent to our study of the non-student's access to the campus is the student's "right to hear." "Freedom to speak would be a hollow right if a concomitant right to hear the speech did not exist."[27]

Springing from the First Amendment right to free speech, the right to hear protects the listener. It is vital that this constitutional right be secured; otherwise a powerful government could guarantee "free speech" but restrict that speech to areas where no one could hear it. Free speech in such a setting would be a vacuous right without any meaningful validity. Since the state school system itself can develop into a closed system with only those faculty members paid by the state teaching and speaking, then the students become a captive audience to those particular points of view approved by the state university public school system. It is in this context that the United States Supreme Court in the *Tinker* case stated:

> In our system, state-operated schools may not be enclaves of totalitarianism. School officials do not possess authority over their students. Students in school as well as out of school are "persons" under our Constitution. They are possessed of fundamental rights which the state must respect. . . . In our system, students may not be regarded as closed-circuit recipients of only that which the State chooses to communicate.[28]

As a consequence, the Supreme Court has been careful to recognize in numerous cases the inherent right of individuals to receive information.[29] Moreover, the right to hear has been recognized in the federal courts as a right possessed by high school students.[30]

The student's right to hear speech is also to be viewed in light of the two-pronged *Tinker* test. In this context, the right to hear could come into play in various situations.

One way would be the presence of a non-student or off-campus speaker who is invited to address a student organization (that is, a university or a high school club). The fact that the lecture may include religious content would not seem to disrupt the orderly operation of the school. Furthermore, the rights of others would not be violated in such a setting since student organizations are voluntary in nature. In other words, anyone present would be there of his own accord, and no coercion on the part of the high school or university would be evident. Therefore, under constitutional analysis the student's right to hear makes the banning of such off-campus speakers by school officials constitutionally suspect.

The Public Forum and Equal Protection of the Laws
In the 1972 case of *Police Department v. Mosley*[31] the Supreme Court announced a constitutional right fashioned from the First Amendment freedoms and the equal protection clause which has come to be known as the "freedom of public forum." This unanimous decision involved the validity of a city ordinance which forbade picketing within 150 feet of a public school building except for picketing in connection with labor disputes. Because the ordinance discriminated against nonlabor-dispute picketing on the basis of *subject matter,* the Court held the ordinance to be invalid:

[U]nder the Equal Protection Clause, not to mention the First Amendment itself, government may not grant the use of a forum to people whose views it finds acceptable, but deny use to those wishing to express less favored or more controversial views. And it may not select which issues are worth discussing or debating in public facilities. . . . Once a forum is opened up to assembly or speaking by some groups, government may not prohibit others from assembling or speaking on the basis of what they intend to say. Selective exclusions from a public forum may not be based on content alone, and may not be justified by reference to content alone.[32]

The Court acknowledged the legitimacy of the city's concern for preventing school disruption, but noted that the ordinance itself, since it did permit some types of picketing, acknowledged that peaceful picketing would not unduly interfere with the school's operation.[33]

Some early court decisions recognized that the public high school can be a public forum.[34] In *Tinker,* of course, the Supreme Court went far beyond such cases by recognizing students' First Amendment rights *during* school hours.[35]

Since the *Tinker* decision, the lower federal courts have applied the public forum rationale in various contexts, including public high schools.[36] For example, in *Lawrence University Bicentennial Commission v. City of Appleton*[37] a federal district court held that a school board guideline which prohibited the use of a public high school for "religious" or political activities (unless such activities were nonpartisan or nondenominational) had the effect of regulating speech on the basis of content and was constitutionally impermissible.[38]

Likewise, in *Vail v. Board of Education*[39] a federal district court recognized that if a public high school provides a forum:

> [I]t must do so in a manner consistent with constitutional principles. Access to the podium must be permitted without discrimination. It is not for the school to control the influence of a public forum by censoring the ideas, the proponents, or the audience. The right of the student to hear a speaker cannot be left to the discretion of school authorities on a pick and choose basis.[40]

Recently, in *Widmar v. Vincent*[41] the Supreme Court, in ruling that a university regulation prohibiting student religious groups to meet on campus was unconstitutional, stated:

> Through its policy of accommodating their meetings, the University has created a forum generally open for use by student groups. Having done so, the University has assumed an obligation to justify its discriminations and exclusions under applicable constitutional norms. The Constitution forbids a State to enforce certain exclusions from a forum generally open to the public, even if it was not required to create the forum in the first place.[42]

Given the fact that the purpose of the First Amendment is to prevent state interference with speech and related freedoms, clearly the state (which includes the public schools) should not be permitted to restrict those views that it dislikes simply because the forum is one it has itself created.[43]

Beyond the constitutional right to freedom of a public forum, there exists additional constitutional authority which would reach the same conclusion based entirely upon Fourteenth Amendment equal protection principles.[44] The equal protection clause is an anti-discrimination provision which requires that persons in similar situations must be treated equally under the law. Once a privilege has been extended by school authorities to selected individuals or groups, the same privilege cannot be denied to other individuals or groups solely on the basis of subject matter (this includes what the individuals intend to say or the content of what is to be said to them, again implying the right to hear).

Most universities and public schools allow student organizations to meet (even if the organizations have religious content). A recurrent controversy has arisen, however, when such groups have invited outside speakers to lecture on campus and to touch on religious topics.

The federal courts have addressed this problem and have upheld both the speaker's right to speak and the student organization's right under the Fourteenth Amendment to be treated equally with other student groups on campus.[45] If other student organizations invite speakers onto campus to speak, then when a student organization invites a speaker to lecture on a religious subject, the school authorities must afford the speaker an opportunity to speak, or violate the student group's equal protection rights.

The courts have stressed that public education campuses cannot deny to their students the privilege of inviting outside speakers to speak on campus if the denial is based upon the subject matter of the speaker's lecture.[46] This constitutional principle was specifically applied by a federal district court in *Stacy v. Williams* to campus student groups who invited outside speakers to lecture on religious subjects.[47] This particular court reversed all the regulations of the University of Mississippi which bore on the subject of outside speakers on campus. Among the rules considered by the court was one which provided that the facilities of the school could not be made available for public religious meetings or gatherings to off-campus persons or groups of persons. The court invalidated this regulation by stating:

> But as this regulation can reasonably be construed to mean that no student religious group may invite outside speakers on religious topics, which prohibition would conflict with the Equal Protection Clause, it must be rejected. . . .[48]

The court in *Stacy v. Williams* stated that if school officials are concerned that an outside speaker's lecture may create the impression that the school system endorses his message, then the school can remedy this situation by requiring that before and after the speaker's presentation an announcement be made that the school does not endorse the speaker's statements.[49] Such announcements would remove any assumption of connection between the school system and the content of the speaker's message.

One other issue that has surfaced in the context of the public forum is the freedom of students to distribute literature on the state university or public school campus. As a consequence of the various court decisions, it is evident that literature which is "libelous, obscene, disruptive of school activities, or likely to create substantial disorder, or which invades the rights of others" may be suppressed by public school officials.[50] However, when no such conditions exist, and particularly when the literature is not sponsored by the school district, is not represented as an official school paper, is not financed by public funds, and is not supervised by school faculty, school administrators have no authority to suppress the distribution of literature on the school campus.[51]

School authorities are thus forbidden to *arbitrarily* ban publications from the school campus. For example, in *Quarterman v. Byrd*[52] a federal court of appeals ruled that a public school regulation prohibiting students from distributing printed material without express permission from the administration prior to its distribution was an improper prior restraint. Such a rule or regulation is invalid on its face.

At a minimum there must be a written policy containing criteria to be followed by school officials when determining whether or not to permit the distribution of literature and procedural safeguards (hearing, notice of charges, etc.) to permit review of a denial. Students, the *Quarterman* court held, are protected by the First Amendment and are permitted to distribute publications on campus unless school authorities "can reasonably 'forecast *substantial* disruption of or material interference with school activities' on account of distribution of such material."[53]

Moreover, students may not be coerced to read books which violate their religious beliefs.[54] In *Grove v. Mead School District,*[55] for example, a student assigned to read *The Learning Tree* found the book offensive to her religious beliefs. The court held she did not have to read the book.

Finally, the argument has been made that many of the decisions dealing with students' rights cases concern fact situations at the university level and, therefore, are not applicable to high school students. This argument has been met and rebuffed by some courts. For example, in *Scoville v. Board of Education*[56] a federal court held that the "fact that it [the other case] involved a university is of no importance, since the relevant principles and rules apply generally to both high schools and universities."[57]

The truth of the matter is that school authorities at either the high school or college level cannot regulate the content of ideas students may hear. "To do so," one federal judge wrote, "is illegal and thus unconstitutional censorship in its rawest form."[58]

4

The Rights of Faculty

It can hardly be argued that either students or teachers shed their constitutional rights . . . at the schoolhouse gate.

Tinker v. Des Moines Independent School District, 393 U.S. 503, 506 (1969)

The First Amendment, as interpreted and defined by the United States Supreme Court, means that the government has no authority to restrict expression because of "its messages, its ideas, its subject matter, or its content."[1] As the Court has said:

It is the purpose of the First Amendment to preserve an uninhibited marketplace of ideas in which truth will ultimately prevail, rather than to countenance monopolization of that market, whether it be by the government itself or a private licensee.[2]

By limiting the power of the government to interfere with freedom of speech, inquiry, and association (thereby necessitating freedom of expression), the Constitution protects all persons, no matter what their calling—including *teachers*. As Justice William O. Douglas once said:

> [T]he counselor, whether priest, parent or *teacher*, no matter how small his audience—these too are beneficiaries of freedom of expression.[3]

Any "inhibition of freedom of thought, and of action upon thought in the case of teachers brings the safeguards of those amendments [First and Fourteenth] vividly into operation."[4] The safeguarding of the freedom of speech and expression is vital in ensuring that "falsehoods may be exposed through the processes of education and discussion."[5] This is part and parcel of the nation's deep commitment to "safeguarding academic freedom" in the public schools, or what the Supreme Court has called the "marketplace of ideas."[6]

Academic Freedom: The Freedom to Teach

Academic freedom is a special concern of the First Amendment. Essentially, laws or rules that cast a "pall of orthodoxy over the classroom" will not be tolerated under the Constitution.[7]

Needless to say, academic freedom involves and protects both students and faculty. The collective freedom of the faculty member to teach and of the student to learn (the "right to hear") has been labeled "academic freedom."[8] This right affords the high school and university teacher broad discretion in choosing study materials, even to the point of defying higher school authorities.[9] Academic freedom allows the teacher liberty to utilize appropriate methods, materials, and means in approaching the curricular subject matter which he or she is assigned to teach. This freedom is invariably protected at the college level,[10] as well as at the public high school level.[11]

Although the *Tinker* decision spoke directly to the rights of students, the Supreme Court also recognized the rights of faculty on the campus.[12] Following the *Tinker* decision in 1972, a federal court in *James v. Board of Education*[13] applied the *Tinker* test to a high school teacher's freedom of expression as guaranteed in the First Amendment.[14]

In the *James* case, as a form of religious expression a high school teacher who held to the Quaker faith wore a black armband into the classroom to protest the Vietnam war. The court upheld this form of expression as being within the ambit of academic freedom in that it did not in any way disrupt the orderly operation of the school or classroom.[15] The court stated:

> [W]e cannot countenance school authorities arbitrarily censoring a teacher's speech merely because they do not agree with the teacher's political philosophies or leanings.[16]

Under the First Amendment, school officials cannot suppress expression of beliefs and feelings with which they do not wish to contend,[17] nor can they constitutionally abridge freedom of speech, or press to obviate slight inconveniences or annoyances.[18] The Supreme Court in *Healy v. James*[19] held without equivocation that school officials cannot restrict the rights of speech and association of either students or faculty simply because they find the views expressed by the group to be abhorrent.[20]

Although the government has the prerogative of prescribing the curriculum for the public schools, it may not "impose upon the teachers in its schools any conditions that it chooses, however restrictive they may be of constitutional guarantees."[21] As one federal court of appeals has held:

> There is little room . . . in the majestic generalities of the Bill of Rights . . . for an interpretation of the First Amendment that would be more restrictive with respect to teachers than it is with respect to their students, where there has been no interference with the requirements of appropriate discipline in the operation of the school.[22]

In *James v. Board of Education*,[23] the court held that teachers are free to make known at school their positions on subjects about which they feel strongly—even if they are religious views. It is recognized, however, that academic freedom is not an absolute right.[24] In this respect, the *James* court noted that teachers are not free to indoctrinate students concerning their views.[25] This means that the teacher should sustain the concept that the classroom is the marketplace of ideas by presenting subject matter objectively. One excellent method of presenting course material objectively is by having outside speakers present a topic from a particular point of view.

The Non-Student Medium for Teaching

In the seminal case of *Wilson v. Chancellor*[26] the issues concerning the non-student's access to the public high school campus were addressed. In this 1976 case a federal court held that a public high school board of education order banning "all political speakers" from access to the school campus was unconstitutional because the order infringed on the student's "right to hear."[27] Most importantly, however, the court ruled that the order was violative of the teacher's freedom of expression by affecting his use of speakers as a medium of teaching.[28] Furthermore, the court ruled that the order violated the teacher's Fourteenth Amendment right to equal protection of the laws and that the order existed to silence an unpopular viewpoint (in this case, the Communist viewpoint).[29]

The *Wilson* case recognizes that the methods and medium utilized to teach a course are included within the teacher's right to academic freedom.[30] The court stated:

> The act of teaching is a form of expression, and the methods used in teaching are media. Wilson's (the teacher) use of . . . speakers was his medium for teaching. . . .[31]

The court in the *Wilson* decision applied the two-part *Tinker* test to the fact situation where a teacher invites an off-campus speaker into the classroom. After careful analysis, the court found no material disruptions in classroom work or invasions of the rights of others.[32] The court held that simply espousing an unpopular viewpoint was no reason to restrict a speaker from the classroom.[33] The court said:

> [N]either fear of voter reaction nor personal disagreement with views to be expressed justifies a suppression of free expression, at least in the absence of any reasonable fear of material and substantial interference with the educational process.[34]

In *Wilson* the right to espouse the Communist viewpoint was upheld as within constitutional parameters. Surely there is no constitutional parameter which would restrict the right of a non-student to lecture on a religious topic, in an otherwise objective context, on the public school campus. This is especially so in light of the teacher's right to use non-student speakers as a medium of teaching.

Teacher Action as State Action: Academic Freedom as Private Conduct

In considering whether any given religious activity is a violation of the First Amendment's prohibition against the establishment of religion, there must be "state action" which in some way implicates the state in initiating or sponsoring a religion.[35] The question is: Since a teacher is a state employee, if the teacher exercises his or her right to religious expression or, let us say, invites a speaker into the classroom to lecture on a religious topic, does this amount to state action? As previously discussed, a religion is impermissibly established when the state (in the form of the public schools) initiates and sponsors religious activity.

There are few cases directly deciding the issue of whether or not "teacher action" is "state action."[36] One federal circuit court of appeals alluded to this issue in its decision and stated the principle that "teacher action" can only be "state action" "if the State has been significantly involved by [the teacher's] actions."[37]

The application of this principle is well illustrated by *James v. Board of Education.*[38] In review, the teacher in this case wore a black armband into the classroom as a religious protest against the Vietnam war. The federal court upheld his actions as falling within the realm of academic freedom. There was no question that Mr. James was expressing only his own personal religious beliefs in the classroom. In fact Mr. James, a practicing Quaker, testified that his action "was 'an expression of [his] religious aversion to war.' "[39]

The *James* case demonstrates that by no stretch of the imagination is "teacher action" always "state action." The doctrine of academic freedom negates the argument that the teacher is merely an agent of the state. Academic freedom allows the teacher broad discretion within the classroom to express himself and to plan the medium through which he is to teach his class.

The conclusion is that such expression on the part of the teacher is private action, not state action. Within the confines of academic freedom, therefore, teacher action does not necessarily implicate the state.

There are circumstances in which school authorities would violate the constitutional freedom of the instructor if they ordered the teacher to cease from discussing religion at all in the classroom. As various federal courts have held, administrative censorship "has an unmistakable tendency to chill that free play of the spirit which all teachers ought especially to cultivate and practice."[40] Moreover, the Supreme Court has said that the danger of a "chilling effect upon the exercise of vital First Amendment rights must be guarded against by sensitive tools which clearly inform teachers what is being proscribed."[41]

Concerning the presentation of religious material in the classroom (or even secular subject matter) by the teacher or an off-campus speaker, such subject matter must be relevant to that which is being taught.[42] To be quite frank, relevancy is rarely a problem, as outside speakers are usually invited into the classroom only because what they have to say is relevant to the course being taught.

5

The Rights of Non-Students

> Once a forum is opened up to assembly or speaking by
> some groups, government may not prohibit others
> from assembling or speaking on the basis of what they
> intend to say.
>
> *Police Department of Chicago u Mosley,*
> 408 U.S. 92, 96 (1972)

Although the rights of non-students to have access
to the university or public school campus are intimately
intertwined with the rights of students and faculty, non-
students do possess rights independent of these two
classes of persons which would support their right to
access.

Freedom of a Public Forum and Equal Protection of the Laws

As discussed in Chapter 3, the freedom of a public
forum, coupled with the Fourteenth Amendment guarantee of equal protection under the laws, affords and
opens, to some extent, the university or public school
campus to non-student or off-campus speakers. Comparable to and supportive of the freedom of a public fo-

rum is a recent line of cases dealing with the access of a particular religious group (Hare Krishna) to a public forum in order to exercise its freedoms of speech and association.[1] These cases, which have been favorable to the adherents of Hare Krishna, have revolved around the breadth of various statutes and ordinances which unconstitutionally restricted their rights and freedoms.

As discussed earlier, First Amendment freedoms are not absolute. They may be restricted if there are compelling state interests. However, the Supreme Court has mandated that in order to justify suppression of those freedoms there must be reasonable grounds to fear that there exists grave and immediate danger to interests which the state may lawfully protect.[2] The danger must be clear and present, not doubtfully or remotely threatening.[3]

Any state statute or ordinance affecting these precious rights must be narrowly drawn so as not to infringe upon these protected rights.[4] Likewise, the First Amendment does not permit the state to restrict the speech of some elements or classes of society in order to enhance the relative voice of others.[5] Indeed, inhibition as well as prohibition against the exercise of First Amendment rights is a power denied to governmental bodies (such as state universities or public schools).[6]

Applying these principles, no compelling state interest justifies prohibiting the non-student who speaks on a religious topic access to the university or public school campus—absent a showing of some clear and present danger to an interest the state must protect. In

Widmar v. Vincent,[7] a university claimed that a clear and present danger existed in their denial of a religious student organization the right to meet on their campus. The university argued that in complying with its duty to avoid establishing a religion, it had to deny access to the campus to religious organizations, even student-sponsored ones.[8] The Supreme Court rebuffed this argument by stating: "It does not follow. . . that an 'equal access' policy would be incompatible with this Court's Establishment Clause cases."[9] Furthermore, the Court said:

> The University has opened its facilities for use by student groups, and the question is whether it can now exclude groups because of the content of their speech.
> . . . In this context we are unpersuaded that the primary effect of the public forum, open to all forms of discourse, would be to advance religion.[10]

It cannot be denied that school officials must operate their schools in orderly fashion and must avoid substantial disruption of the educational process. However, as Justice William Powell said in the Supreme Court's decision in *Healy v. James:*[11]

> Yet, the precedents of this court leave no room for the view that, because of the acknowledged need for order, First Amendment protections should apply with less force on the college campuses than in the community at large. Quite to the contrary, "[t]he vigilant protection of constitutional freedoms is nowhere more vital than in the community of American schools."[12]

Once the state (in the form of the university or public school system) opens its facilities to certain groups, it cannot *arbitrarily* prevent any members of the public from holding such meetings. As stated by a federal district court in ·*Vail v. Board of Education*,[13] if the public high school provides a forum

> [I]t must do so in a manner consistent with constitutional principles. Access to the podium must be permitted without discrimination. It is not for the school to control the influence of a public forum by censoring the ideas, the proponents, or the audience. The right of the student to hear a speaker cannot be left to the discretion of school authorities on a pick and choose basis.[14]

If *one* group or *one* speaker is allowed onto the campus to speak in classrooms or to assembled students, then the campus becomes an open forum.[15] Although the school authorities may *reasonably* regulate the speech as to time, place and manner,[16] they may not *arbitrarily* discriminate against a non-student off-campus speaker because the school authorities dislike the content of the speaker's lecture or speech.

This principle is well illustrated in *Lawrence University Bicentennial Commission v. City of Appleton*[17] and in *Country Hills Christian Church v. Unified School District No. 512.*[18] In these two cases federal district courts ruled that school board guidelines which prohibited the use of public high schools for religious activities had the effect of regulating speech on the basis of content and were constitutionally impermissible.[19]

Although the constitutional right to freedom of a public forum has equal protection overtones, there are also cases which reach the same conclusion entirely upon pure equal protection clause principles. As mentioned earlier, the Fourteenth Amendment equal protection clause provides that persons must be treated equally under the law.

As discussed in Chapter Three, a federal court in *Stacy v. Williams*[20] reviewed all the rules of the University of Mississippi which bore on the subject of outside speakers on campus. Among the rules considered by the court, one provided that facilities of the university could not be made available for public religious meetings to off-campus persons or groups of persons.[21] The court struck down this regulation as being violative of the Fourteenth Amendment equal protection clause.[22]

Stacy v. Williams clearly illustrates that "religion" is not a reasonable classification and that a state may not choose the broad classification of "religion" for exclusion in its public education institutions. To do so violates the rights of non-students to access to a public forum and equal protection under the laws.

The prior restraint on the freedom of expression is also present in the situation where off-campus speakers are banned because of what they may say. Although prior restraints are not unconstitutional per se, their invalidity is heavily presumed.[23] The state simply cannot censor and restrain speech as to content before there is a chance to express oneself, unless there exists a substantial constitutional reason to do so. Such "substantial constitutional reasons" for restraining speech, however, are extremely rare.

6

The Equal Access Act

"[The Equal Access Act] means the school will have the [same] regulations for a religious club as for any other club, no more, no less."

Senator Mark Hatfield

President Reagan signed the Equal Access Act into law on August 11, 1984. The Act was designed by Congress to clarify and confirm the rights of free speech, freedom of association, and the free exercise of religion, as well as other constitutional rights that accrue to public secondary school students.

Congress intended that the Act would restrain public school officials from any discriminatory censorship of speech with religious content. In the words of Senator Jeremiah Denton: "[E]qual access legislation is necessary because school administrators have felt constrained to prohibit and have cancelled voluntary student meetings for such reason that the speech contains religious content."[1] Senator Orrin Hatch echoed similar sentiments. He noted that "religious students are being told they cannot meet on the same basis as other clubs."[2] Senator Mark Hatfield, as well, affirmed the principle of equal treatment, stating that equal access "means the school will have the [same] regulations for a religious club as for any other club, no more, no less."[3]

The equal access principle, as originally conceptualized, resolved that public school policies should be *content neutral*—that is, discrimination based on content of speech (even religious speech) would be prohibited. Under the Act, then, school officials are required to afford equal rights not only to traditional student groups (such as the chess club, drama club, science club, etc.), but also to students desiring to form clubs with religious themes or content.

School officials, of course, retain the authority to establish reasonable time, place, and manner restrictions on student activities. The Equal Access Act simply requires a nondiscriminatory application of the rules.[4]

The Hostility Problem

During committee hearings on equal access, Congress heard testimony by secondary school students, representing various states, that evidenced a pattern of hostility toward and discrimination against those who would exercise their constitutional rights in the public school context. Lisa Bender, named plaintiff in *Bender v. Williamsport Area School District*,[5] submitted to the Senate Judiciary Committee a letter from her high school's school board. That letter denied the right of a voluntary student club, "Petros," to meet on an equal basis with other student groups. Her response was,

"[W]e saw in the Constitution that our freedom of speech was being denied us."[6]

Judy Jankowski of St. Paul, Minnesota, also testified:

> A few years ago, I visited Poland with my family. We stayed with a family that we have [sic] five children in school. I observed how restricted they were to express themselves politically and religiously, and I was thankful that I lived in the United States and that I had the freedom to express myself and share political and religious beliefs with others.
>
> Now, and just a few years later, I see the same restrictions put on me and my fellow classmates that are on the students in Poland, and I find this very disturbing.[7]

Bonnie Bailey of Lubbock, Texas, explained her feelings to the Committee by stating:

> We have been taught that the Constitution guarantees us freedom of speech. But we feel that here we have been discriminated against, because we can picket, we can demonstrate, we can curse, we can take God's name in vain, but we cannot voluntarily get together and talk about God on any part of our campus, inside or out of the school.
>
> We just feel frustrated because we don't feel like we are being treated equally.[8]

Stuart McKinney, from an Atlanta, Georgia, suburb, explained:

At North Clayton Junior High School, only religious clubs were singled out for discrimination, although there were many other clubs:

> North Clayton Junior High School offers students a wide range of extracurricular activities. These include the drama club, the beta club, FHA, math and science club, newspaper staff, student council, letterman's clubs, language clubs, chess club, plus a wide variety of sports related activities.

> Membership in all of these clubs are . . . voluntary, yet none of the clubs above were . . . affected as the Youth for Christ Club.[9]

Bonnie Bailey added:

> At Monterey High School in Lubbock, Texas, for example, neither Y-Teens, an organization sponsored by Y.W.C.A. and open to all girls regardless of their religious beliefs, nor Tri-H-Y, which is sponsored by Y.M.C.A., can hold any activities on school grounds, including benefit dances for the American Cancer Society.[10]

Prior to passage of the Equal Access Act, students such as these faced three important hurdles in their attempt to enjoy full protection of their First Amendment rights under the Constitution. The first was the discretion exercised by school administrators who are often confused concerning the rights of religious students, and requests for equal treatment. Students and parents often felt helpless as they petitioned school board attorneys who were either uninformed about the First Amendment or who, fearing costly litigation, were overly conservative in their interpretation of the law or who often relied on the advice of public interest groups opposed to free religious expression in the public schools. In the words of Peter Eagon of Snohomish, Washington, "Recently an assembly featuring professional athletes speaking about what has been an important part of their lives and what has made them successful was denied because it was held to be too religious to be held during school hours by the A.C.L.U."[11]

The activities of such groups as the American Civil Liberties Union (ACLU), coupled with a confused and sometimes hostile school administration, often proved insurmountable to an unprotected student with limited resources. Even school boards favorable to religious student rights are persuaded by tight budgets and other tensions to give in to pressures from interest groups. In short, it was easier to say no to the students. This is perhaps one of the problems that the concept of the Equal Access Act seeks to remedy.

The second hurdle was that students and their parents, as novices in civil rights matters, often faced the difficult, if not impossible, task of locating attorneys to defend religious student rights. Equal Access legislation was originally designed to solve this problem by encouraging United States attorneys to assist indigent students where a genuine case developed.[12]

Third, even if a student finds a competent attorney, there are conflicting federal circuit court decisions on various aspects of the equal access question, some of which take a narrow view of the First Amendment rights of students. Congress sought to overcome these hurdles through the Equal Access Act by codifying constitutional rights and by placing remedial measures within the students' reach.

The Equal Access Act

In light of the problems discussed above, it is appropriate to examine the Equal Access Act. The following is a succinct sectional analysis of the Act.

> *TITLE VIII—THE EQUAL ACCESS ACT*
> *Short Title*
> *SEC. 801. This title may be cited*
> *as "The Equal Access Act."*

> *DENIAL OF EQUAL ACCESS PROHIBITED*
> *SEC. 802. (a) It shall be unlawful for any public secondary school which receives Federal financial assistance and which has a limited open forum to deny equal access or a fair opportunity to, or discriminate against, any students who wish to conduct a meeting within that limited open forum on the basis of the religious, political, philosophical, or other content of the speech at such meetings.*
>
> *(b) A public secondary school has a limited open forum whenever such a school grants an offering to or opportunity for one or more noncurriculum related student groups to meet on school premises during noninstructional time.*

This section of the Act sets forth the fundamental equal treatment requirement that the Act places on public secondary schools. The Act is limited to those public schools that receive federal financial assistance. There are very few, if any, public schools that do not receive such assistance. Thus, the Act virtually applies universally to all such schools.

The Act applies to the "secondary schools"—the definition of which is left within the discretion of state law. Generally, secondary schools comprise grades 9 through 12, although some states define such schools as making up grades 7 through 12 or 10 through 12.

The phrase "to deny equal access or a fair opportunity to, or discriminate against" means that within the "limited open forum" the rights of all students should be on an equal basis. This includes religious students.

The phrase "conduct a meeting" is broad. It recognizes that whatever is actually permitted by schools should pertain to student groups equally.

The last phrase of section 802(a) ("on the basis of the religious, political, philosophical, or other content of speech at such meetings") includes not only religious speech, but applies to all forms of speech. This conforms with the United States Supreme Court decision in *Widmar v. Vincent*[13] which indicated that religious speech, including worship, has the same status as other types of speech.

One of the most important phrases in the Act is the concept of the "limited open forum." It may be more restrictive of the constitutional rights and freedoms of secondary school students than the Constitution mandates. Let me explain.

The existence and status of a "limited open forum" depends on the phrase in section 802(b) which states, "whenever such school grants" such a forum. This clause is permissive. It leaves it to the discretion of the public secondary school whether or not it will have a "limited open forum." Thus, a school is ostensibly free to adjust its forum to where it will not permit any such forum. *Tinker* and other similar cases, however, are not this restrictive of First Amendment rights. Therefore, under the *Tinker* doctrine (discussed in detail in Chapter 3), restrictions on speech, as a result of closing a limited public forum, could render at least part of the Act unconstitutional.

Section (b) defines a limited open forum as existing when the school allows "one or more noncurriculum related student groups to meet on school premises during noninstructional time." Therefore, if the equal access principle of the Act is to apply, the student groups must be unrelated to the curriculum.

The phrase "noncurriculum related student groups" is left undefined in the Act. However, in section 803(3) the term "meeting" is defined to include activities "not directly related to the school curriculum."

Whenever one of the terms of a congressional enactment is left undefined within the law itself, the legislative history often provides the intended meaning. Unfortunately, if called into question, a court studying the legislative history of the Equal Access Act will note the lack of clarity over the exact meaning of the terms "noncurriculum related." However, several senators, including Mark Hatfield, agreed that local school districts would retain the authority to draw the line between curriculum related and noncurriculum related activities.[14] It is also significant that meetings "indirectly" related to the curriculum are not proscribed.

Moreover, the limited open forum concept appears to apply only to "noninstructional time." This is defined in section 803(4) of the Act to mean "time set aside by the school before actual classroom instruction begins or after classroom instruction ends." Thus, any time during noninstructional hours (before or after school, lunch time, free periods, study halls, etc.), the student should be free to choose to participate in extra-curricular activities—even if they have religious content.

It must be emphasized that on the question of whether religious groups (or other groups) may meet in a limited open forum during the school day, supporters of the Act were openly divided. However, from the face of the Act it seems that such meetings should be allowed. Obviously, a court decision in favor of allowing such activities during the school day would be more consistent with the ultimate equal access principle of the Act.

Section 802(c)

(c) Schools shall be deemed to offer a fair opportunity to students who wish to conduct a meeting within its limited open forum if such school uniformly provides that—

(1) the meeting is voluntary and student-initiated;

(2) there is no sponsorship of the meeting by the school, the government, or its agents or employees;

(3) employees or agents of the school or government are present at religious meetings only in a nonparticipatory capacity;

(4) the meeting does not materially and substantially interfere with the orderly conduct of educational activities within the school; and

(5) nonschool persons may not direct, conduct, control, or regularly attend activities of student groups.

The "fair opportunity" requirement of section (a) is mandatory if the Act is to be applied within a limited open forum to a particular school. If any of the five subparagraphs of section (c) are *not* provided for by the school, then a fair opportunity does not exist and the school is in violation of the Act.

Under sections 802(c)(1) and (2) the meeting must be voluntary, student-initiated events with no "sponsorship" by "the school, the government, or its agents or employees." Moreover, section (c)(3) mandates that employees or agents of the school (or government) may be present at "religious meetings only in a nonparticipatory capacity."

Sponsorship is defined in section 803(2) as including "the act of promoting, leading, or participating in a meeting." The school must require that no school or government official promote, lead, or participate in any student meeting in the school's limited open forum. This requirement may or may not mean that the school could not announce or endorse the meetings being held. However, if announcements are given for some extracurricular activities, then the principle of equal access would mandate that announcements be made for all. The paragraph does not require that a teacher or other school employee could not be present at meetings to keep order. Section 803(2) expressly allows such presence for *"custodial purposes."*

Under section 802(c)(3) employees or agents of the school or government may be present at religious meetings "only in a nonparticipatory capacity." The Act's provision concerning participation by teachers or other school employees leaves open the question whether their active participation would carry the imprimatur of state approval. Previous concerns in this area have related to formal classroom instruction. It is unclear whether a student-initiated invitation to anybody to participate in their meetings would violate the First Amendment, particularly the student's right to hear. In addition, the First Amendment rights of teachers may be violated by such a narrow interpretation. In any event, the Act permits a teacher to be present as a "monitor," responsible for ensuring good order and the protection of school property.

Section 802(c)(4) provides that the meeting must not "materially and substantially interfere with the orderly conduct of educational activities within the school." The language of this section is adopted from the United States Supreme Court's 1969 decision in *Tinker v. Des Moines Independent Community School Dis-*

trict.[15] The Court held in that case that high school students may express themselves throughout the school day, even on controversial issues, as long as the expression does not "materially and substantially interfer[e] with the requirements of appropriate discipline in the operation of the school."[16] Therefore, the Equal Access Act does not seek to expand the scope of students' free speech rights any further than the limits previously established by the United States Supreme Court.

Section (c)(5) provides that "nonschool persons may not direct, conduct, control, or regularly attend activities of student groups." Nonschool persons can mean various categories of nonstudents including youth workers, parents, and students from schools other than the school in which a student group is meeting. This requirement is an attempt to ensure that student groups be initiated, directed, conducted, and controlled by students only. In light of the rights of nonstudents, as discussed in Chapter 5, this section is too restrictive and may be constitutionally suspect.

Section 802(d)

(d) Nothing in this title shall be construed to authorize the United States or any State or political subdivision thereof—

(1) to influence the form or content of any prayer or other religious activity;

(2) to require any person to participate in prayer or other religious activity;

(3) to expend public funds beyond the incidental cost of providing the space for student-initiated meetings;

(4) to compel any school agent or employee to attend a school meeting if the content of the speech at the meeting is contrary to the beliefs of the agent or employee;
(5) to sanction meetings that are otherwise unlawful;
(6) to limit the rights of groups of students which are not of a specified numerical size; or
(7) to abridge the constitutional rights of any person.

In this section of the Equal Access Act public schools are not authorized to do certain things. Neither does the Act specifically prohibit the topics covered in section 802(d). However, we might say that a *constitutional caution* is raised in this section.

The congressional concerns aired in this section are rather straightforward. The key words may be "require," "compel," "unlawful," "limit," "abridge," and so on.

Two principles, then, emerge from this section. The first is the need to protect the rights of all, students and non-students, within the corridors of the public schools. Thus, all the meetings contemplated under the Act must be voluntary and without coercion from school authorities or the government. Second, the issue of state sponsorship is raised in section (d)(3). The emphasis here is equal access, not unequal, discriminatory, or superior access.

Finally, the Act protects voluntary student-initiated activity wherein students are seeking to meet with other students. As such, the Act should not be interpreted to violate or curtail the constitutional rights of students below the secondary level or the rights of teachers or non-students.

Sections 802(e) and (f)

(e) *Notwithstanding the availability of any other remedy under the Constitution or the laws of the United States, nothing in this title shall be construed to authorize the United States to deny or withhold Federal financial assistance to any school.*

(f) *Nothing in this Act shall be construed to limit the authority of the school, its agents or employees, to maintain order and discipline on school premises, to protect the well-being of students and faculty, and to assure that attendance of students at meetings is voluntary.*

The Equal Access Act does not authorize the withholding or denial of federal financial assistance to any public school. Therefore, anyone aggrieved under the Act must turn to the courts for relief. This means lawsuits based upon violations of the Act itself and/or the constitutional theories set forth in this book.

Section 802(f) makes it clear that Congress by way of the Act was not attempting in any way to diminish the role of the schools "to maintain order and discipline" and to protect students and teachers. This section again raises the congressional concern for the voluntary nature of the activities protected by the Act. Thus, if necessary, school authorities could take *reasonable* steps to assure voluntariness of student meetings covered by the Act.

DEFINITIONS

SEC. 803. *As used in this title—*

(1) The term "secondary school" means a public school which provides secondary education as determined by State law

(2) The term "sponsorship" includes the act of promoting, leading, or participating in a meeting. The assignment of a teacher, administrator, or other school employee to a meeting for custodial purposes does not constitute sponsorship of the meeting.

(3) The term "meeting" includes those activities of student groups which are permitted under a school's limited open forum and are not directly related to the school curriculum.

(4) The term "noninstructional time" means time set aside by the school before actual classroom instruction begins or after actual classroom instruction ends.

SEVERABILITY

SEC. 804. *If any provision of this title or the application thereof to any person or circumstances is judicially determined to be invalid, the provisions of the remainder of the title and the application to other persons or circumstances shall not be affected thereby.*

CONSTRUCTION

SEC. 805. *The provisions of this title shall supersede all other provisions of Federal law that are inconsistent with the provisions of this title.*

These remaining sections are self-explanatory and were discussed earlier under the appropriate section.

Conclusion

Obviously, those interested in promoting and preserving freedom of religious expression in public secondary schools should familiarize themselves with the Act.

Students and others interested in meeting as a group on school premises should determine whether the school has a limited open forum. If the school does not have a limited open forum, the Act does not apply.

If the school has a limited open forum, school officials should be contacted by those interested to find out what written procedures are necessary as a prerequisite to meeting. If there are no written procedures, inquire as to the school's past practices. If the procedures are reasonably within the parameters of the Act and do not violate the Constitution, then steps should be taken to comply with them.

If, however, it is clear that school officials are violating both the Constitution and the Act, they should be so notified. And if upon notice of violations, they refuse to follow the mandates of the law, then legal action should be considered.

Often it is important to appeal injustice. Sometimes it is *necessary* in order to ensure liberty and preserve an open and free society.

7

The Open Society

Our peculiar security is in possession of a written Constitution. Let us not make it a blank paper by construction.

Thomas Jefferson

The liberties of expression, association, religion, the freedom of a public forum, and the right to the equal protection of the laws are in a sense all components of the right of citizens to open communication. What is the value of these communication rights?

It might be argued that to deny religious expression in the public school does not completely destroy the right of religious communication. Rather, it merely restricts the time and place of the communication. Further, it might be argued that only one subject matter is eliminated, leaving communication perfectly open on all other subjects.

Similar arguments were made to the United States Supreme Court in the case of *Thomas v. Collins*.[1] There a labor union officer was held in contempt of a court order prohibiting him from soliciting union members without first registering with the state. The state unsuccessfully contended that it was a small thing to ask him to register. The Supreme Court held that "[t]he restraint is not small when it is considered what was restrained,"[2] and emphasized that "it is the character of the right, not of the limitation"[3] which is placed upon the scales of justice.

With respect to the argument that religious expression by students, teachers, and non-students can be had at another time and place, the Supreme Court in deciding *Schneider v. State*[4] proclaimed that "one is not to have the exercise of his liberty of expression in appropriate places abridged on the plea that it may be exercised in some other place."[5] Likewise, in the case of *Healy v. James*[6] the Supreme Court reiterated the importance of student associational freedoms:

> [T]he [student] group's possible ability to exist outside the campus community does not ameliorate significantly the disabilities imposed by [the failure to recognize the group as an official campus organization]. We are not free to disregard the practical realities.[7]

The practical realities are that if students are to communicate with other students on any subject, they must do it where students come together—*at school.*

At the high school and university level the rights presently held by teachers and students are substantial. The teacher's constitutional right to academic freedom and the student's right to hear both provide a strong and durable constitutional base from which a nonstudent may gain access to the campus.

School officials do not have a compelling state interest in denying an off-campus speaker access to the campus simply because he or she plans to speak on a religious topic. To the contrary, as the United States Supreme Court has held, the state must accommodate religious freedom in such instances.

The classroom has been said to be the marketplace of ideas. As long as material is relevant to the subject matter being taught and is taught in an otherwise objective context, it is suggested that school authorities should perpetuate this concept and maintain the freedoms essential to a proper administration of the education system.

We live in a nation today where young men and women are exposed to a great amount of data and as a result are maturing at a much earlier age. The time has passed when it can be validly argued that the young must be shielded. Instead, they must be provided with an adequate educational base from which to confront a world that abounds with devastating crises.

One effective way of providing such an educational base is by allowing freedom of religious expression. In this way, not only can the educational objective be attained, but also precious liberties of antiquity can be preserved.

Notes

Chapter One

1. Terry Eastland, "In Defense of Religious America," *Commentary* (June 1981), p. 40.
2. H. Commager, Preface, in *McGuffey's Fifth Eclectic Reader*.
3. Robert Cord, *Separation of Church and State: Historical Fact and Current Fiction* (New York: Lambeth Press, 1982), pp. 23, 253.
4. *Marsh v. Chambers,* 463 U.S. 783 (1983).
5. Cord, *supra* note 3, at 27-29.
6. *Ibid.*
7. *Ibid.*, pp. 29-36.
8. *Ibid.*, pp. 37-39.
9. J. O. Wilson, *Public Schools of Washington,* Vol. 1, Records of the Columbia Historical Society (1897), p. 4.
10. *Ibid.*, p. 5.
11. *Ibid.*, p. 6.
12. *See Jaffree v. Wallace,* 105 S. Ct. 2479, 2508 (1985) (Rehnquist, J., dissenting).
13. 1 *Annals of Congress* (Gales and Seaton, ed., 1834), p. 454.

Chapter Two

1. 104 S. Ct. 1355 (1984).
2. *Ibid.* at 1359 (emphasis supplied; footnotes omitted).
3. 105 S. Ct. 2479 (1985). *See also Walter v. West Virginia,* 610 F. Supp. 1169 (S.D. W. Va. 1985).
4. *Ibid.* at 2483. *See also Aguillard v. Edwards,* 765 F.2d 1251 (5th Cir. 1985), 57 U.S.L.W. 3724 (May 6, 1986), wherein a statute was invalidated which required the teaching of creation-science whenever the theory of evolution was taught because the statute's primary purpose was to advance a religious doctrine.

5. *Zorach v. Clauson,* 343 U.S. 306, 314 (1952).
6. *See e.g., Zorach v. Clauson,* 343 U.S. 306 (1952); *Engel v. Vitale,* 370 U.S. 421 (1962); *School District of Abington Township, Pa. v. Schempp,* 374 U.S. 203 (1963); *Walz v. Tax Commission,* 397 U.S. 664 (1970); and, *Roemer v. Board of Public Works of Maryland,* 426 U.S. 736 (1976).
7. 397 U.S. 664 (1970).
8. *Ibid.* at 669 (emphasis supplied).
9. 426 U.S. 736 (1976).
10. *Ibid.* at 745-46 (emphasis supplied).
11. *Lemon v. Kurtzman,* 403 U.S. 602, 612-13, *reh'g denied,* 404 U.S. 876 (1971) (emphasis supplied). The tripartite test, however, has been brought into question in some recent cases. *See generally Marsh v. Chambers,* 463 U.S. 783 (1983); *Lynch v. Donnelly,* 104 S. Ct. 1355 (1984); *See also* discussion of the *Lemon* test in *Mueller v. Allen,* 463 U.S. 388 (1983).
12. 426 U.S. at 747 (emphasis supplied).
13. 333 U.S. 203 (1948).
14. 370 U.S. 421 (1962).
15. 374 U.S. 203 (1963).
16. 449 U.S. 39, *reh'g denied,* 449 U.S. 1104 (1981). The lower federal courts have followed the Supreme Court's example. *See Jaffree v. Wallace,* 705 F.2d 1526 (11th Cir. 1983), prob. juris. noted, 104 S. Ct. 1704 (1984) (statute authorizing prayer in public school unconstitutional); *Nartowicz v. Clayton County School District,* 736 F.2d 646 (11th Cir. 1984); *May v. Cooperman,* 572 F. Supp. 156 (C.D. NJ 1983) (statute which provided for observance of one minute of silence at beginning of school day unconstitutional); *Crockett v. Sorenson,* 568 F. Supp. 1422 (W.D. Va. 1983) (public school's Bible program unconstitutional); *Duffy v. Las Cruces Public Schools,* 557 F. Supp. 1013 (D. N. Mex. 1983) (statute allowing moment of silence in public schools unconstitutional); *Karen B. v. Treen,* 653 F.2d 897 (5th Cir. 1981), *aff'd,* 455 U.S. 913 (1982) (statute authorizing voluntary students or teachers to initiate prayer at the beginning of the school day unconstitutional); *Lubbock Civil Liberties Union v. Lubbock Independent School District,* 669 F.2d 1038 (5th Cir. 1982), *cert. denied,* 103 S. Ct. 800 (1983) (school board policy of permitting students to use school facilities either before or after the regular school hours for religious purposes); *Hall v. Board of School Commissioners of Conecuh County,* 656 F.2d 999 (5th Cir. 1981) (conducting morning devotional reading over school's public address system and conducting a course of Bible literature in a manner which advanced religion unconstitution-

al); *Collins v. Chandler Unified School District,* 644 F.2d 759 (1981), *cert. denied,* 454 U.S. 863 (1981) (student council members reciting prayers and Bible verses at school assemblies unconstitutional); *Brandon v. Board of Education of Guilderland Central School District,* 635 F.2d 971 (2d Cir. 1980), *cert. denied,* 454 U.S. 1123 (1981), *reh'g denied,* 455 U.S. 983 (1982) (school's refusal to allow students to meet on school facilities for prayer meetings before or after school held not unconstitutional); *Malnak v. Yogi,* 592 F.2d 197 (3rd Cir. 1979) (teaching course called Science of Creative Intelligence-Transcendental Meditation unconstitutional); *Meltzer v. Board of Public Instruction of Orange County, Florida,* 548 F.2d 559 (5th Cir. 1977), *modified cert. denied,* 439 U.S. 1089 (1978) (distribution of Gideon Bibles, Bible readings on school facilities, and a state statute requiring teachers to "inculcate by precept and example . . . every Christian virtue" unconstitutional); *Depain v. DeKalb County Community School District,* 384 F.2d 836 (7th Cir. 1967), *cert. denied,* 390 U.S. 906 (1968) (prayer recited by class prior to morning snack unconstitutional); *Stein v. Oshinsky,* 348 F.2d 999 (2nd Cir. 1965), *cert. denied,* 382 U.S. 957 (1965) (school officials could constitutionally prevent students from having an opportunity in the classroom for praying); *Goodwin v. Cross Country School District No. 7,* 394 F. Supp. 417 (E.D.Ark.1973) (student council members reading Bible verses and the Lord's Prayer over school intercom and distribution of Gideon Bibles unconstitutional). However, *see Florey v. Sioux Falls School District,* 619 F. 2d 1311 (8th Cir. 1980), *cert. denied,* 449 U.S. 987 (1980) (rules permitting public school Christmas observances with religious elements constitutional); *Reed v. Van Hoven,* 237 F. Supp. 48 (W.D. Mich. 1965) (student-initiated voluntary prayer before commencement of school day constitutional); *ACLU v. Albert Gallatin Area School District,* 307 F. Supp. 637 (W.D. Pa. 1969) (daily Bible readings and recitation of the Lord's Prayer unconstitutional when directed by school authorities).

17. 105 S. Ct. 2479 (1985). *See also May v. Cooperman,* 54 U.S.L.W. 2351 (3rd Cir. 1985).

18. Comment, *Constitutional Law—Religious Exercises and the Public Schools,* 20 Arkansas Law Review 320, 325-26, n. 44 (1967).

19. 374 U.S. at 225.

20. *Ibid.* at 300 (emphasis supplied).

21. *Ibid.* at 306.

22. *Zorach v. Clauson,* 343 U.S. 306, 312-13 (1952). *See also Marsh v. Alabama,* 463 U.S. 783, 792 (1982) (allowing prayer in state legislatures is simply a tolerable acknowledgment of beliefs

widely held among the people of this country); *Wallace v. Jaffree,* 105 S. Ct. 2479, 2507 (1985) (Burger, J., dissenting) ("the religious observances of others should be tolerated, and where possible, accommodated").

23. 374 U.S. at 225 (quoting *Zorach v. Clauson,* 343 U.S. 306, 314 (1952)). *See Crockett v. Sorenson,* 568 F. Supp. 1422, 1425-1426 (W.D. Va. 1983); *Jaffree v. Board of School Commissioners of Mobile County,* 554 F. Supp. 1104, 1108 (S.D. Ala. 1983).

24. 367 U.S. 488 (1961).

25. *Ibid.* at 495, n. 11.

26. Comment, *Humanistic Values in the Public School Curriculum: Problems in Defining an Appropriate "Wall of Separation,"* 61 Northwestern University Law Review 795, 807 (1966).

27. 374 U.S. at 225 (quoting *Zorach v. Clauson,* 343 U.S. 306, 314 (1952).

28. 343 U.S. at 313, 314.

Chapter Three

1. *See e.g., In re Gault,* 387 U.S. 1 (1967).

2. 393 U.S. 503 (1969).

3. *Ibid.* at 505-06.

4. *Ibid.* at 511.

5. *Ibid.* at 513.

6. 454 U.S. 263 (1981). *See Board of Trustees of the Village of Scarsdale v. McCreary,* 739 F.2d 716 (2d Cir. 1984), *aff'd,* 53 U.S.L.W. 4431 (1985), where *Widmar* was applied in upholding the display of a creche in a public park. *Cf. Greater Houston Chapter of American Civil Liberties Union v. Eckels,* 589 F. Supp. 222 (S.D. Tex. 1984); *American Civil Liberties Union v. City of Birmingham,* 588 F. Supp. 1337 (E.D. Mich. 1984); *American Civil Liberties Union of Georgia v. Rabun County Chamber of Commerce,* 698 F.2d 1098 (11th Cir. 1983).

7. *Ibid.* at 265.

8. *Ibid.* at 269. *See also Bender v. Williamsport Area School District,* 106 S. Ct. 1326 (1986) in which the United States Supreme Court vacated and remanded for dismissal the ruling of the Seventh Circuit Court of Appeals for lack of jurisdiction, and reinstated the district court's summary judgment for a group of students seeking to hold a religious meeting during a public high school's activity period.

9. *Ibid.* at 277.

10. 393 U.S. at 512. *See also Stein v. Plainwell Community Schools,* 610 F. Supp. 43 (W.D. Mich. 1985) and *Graham v. Central Community School District of Decatur,* 608 F. Supp. 531 (S.D. Iowa 1985), wherein the district courts held that benediction as part of a graduation program was not an establishment of religion as the program was totally planned by students, was voluntary as attendance was not required to graduate, and occurred only once a year.

11. Murphy, *The Prior Restraint Doctrine in the Supreme Court: A Reevaluation,* 51 Notre Dame Lawyer, 898, 898-99 (1976).

12. 393 U.S. at 514 (emphasis supplied).

13. *See* Comment, *Prior Restraints in Public High Schools,* 82 Yale Law Journal, 1325, 1329, 1333 (1973).

14. *Kunz v. New York,* 340 U.S. 290 (1951).

15. 393 U.S. at 508.

16. Note, 35 Maryland Law Review, 512, 522 (1976).

17. 509 F.2d 652 (1st Cir. 1974). *See also Gay Student Services v. Texas A & M University,* 737 F.2d 1317 (5th Cir. 1984), *cert. denied,* 53 U.S.L.W. 3697 (1985).

18. *Ibid.* at 661 (citing *Police Department of Chicago v. Mosley,* 408 U.S. 92, 95 (1972)).

19. 509 F.2d at 661 (emphasis supplied). *See also Country Hills Christian Church v. Unified School District No. 512,* 560 F. Supp. 1207, 1215 (D. Kan. 1983).

20. 393 U.S. at 511 (emphasis supplied).

21. *NAACP v. Alabama,* 357 U.S. 449, 460 (1958).

22. 408 U.S. 169 (1972).

23. *Ibid.* at 181.

24. In *Scoville v. Board of Education of Joliet Township High School District 204,* 425 F.2d 10, 13, n. 5 (7th Cir. 1970), *cert. denied,* 400 U.S. 826 (1970), the Court of Appeals noted: "The fact that [the other case] involved a university is of no importance, since the relevant principles and rules apply generally to both high schools and universities." *See also Bender v. Williamsport Area School District,* 106 S. Ct. 1326 (1986).

25. 393 U.S. at 512 (emphasis supplied).

26. 509 F.2d at 660 (quoting *NAACP v. Alabama,* 357 U.S. 449, 460 (1958) (emphasis supplied)). *See also Menora v. Illinois High School Association,* 683 F. 2d 1030 (7th Cir. 1982). *But cf. American Future Systems, Inc. v. State University of New York College at Cortland,* 565 F. Supp. 754 (N.D. NY 1983), where distinction is made concerning commercial speech.

27. Comment, *The Right to Receive and the Commercial Speech Doc-*

trine: New Constitutional Considerations, 63 Georgetown Law Journal, 775, 777-778 (1975).
28. 393 U.S. at 511.
29. Comment, *The Right to Receive and the Commercial Speech Doctrine: New Constitutional Considerations,* 63 Georgetown Law Journal, 775, 777-778 (1975). *See e.g., Martin v. City of Struthers,* 319 U.S. 141, 143 (1943); *New York Times Co. v. Sullivan,* 376 U.S. 254, 272 (1964); *Lamont v. Postmaster General,* 381 U.S. 301, 305 (1965); *Griswold v. Connecticut,* 381 U.S. 479, 482 (1965); *Stanley v. Georgia,* 394 U.S. 557, 564 (1969); *Red Lion Broadcasting Co. v. FCC,* 395 U.S. 367, 390 (1969); and, *Linmark Associates, Inc. v. Willingboro, Tp.,* 431 U.S. 85 (1977).
30. *See e.g., Vail v. Board of Education,* 354 F. Supp. 592 (D.N.H. 1973), *vacated,* 502 F. 2d 1159 (1st Cir. 1973); *Wilson v. Chancellor,* 418 F. Supp. 1358 (D. Ore. 1976); and, *Lawrence University Bicentennial Commission v. City of Appleton,* 409 F. Supp. 1319 (E.D. Wis. 1976).
    The student's right to hear has also found federal court approval at the university level. *See e.g., Snyder v. Board of Trustees,* 286 F. Supp. 927, 932 (N.D. Ill., E.D. 1968); *Stacy v. Williams,* 306 F. Supp. 963, 977 (N.D. Miss., W.D., 1969), *aff'd,* 446 F. 2d 1366 (5th Cir., 1971); *Smith v. University of Tennessee,* 300 F. Supp. 777, 780 (E.D. Tenn., N.D. 1969); *Brooks v. Auburn University,* 296 F. Supp. 188, 192, 199 (M.D. Ala. E.D. 1969), *aff'd,* 412 F. 2d 1171 (5th Cir. 1969); *Molpus v. Fortune,* 311 F. Supp. 240, 243, 245 (N.D. Miss., W.D. 1970), aff'd 432 F. 2d 916 (5th Cir. 1970); and, *A.C.L.U. of Virginia v. Radford College,* 315 F. Supp. 893, 896 (W.D. Va. 1970). *Cf. Sheck v. Baileyville School Committee,* 530 F. Supp. 679 (D. Me. 1982).
31. 408 U.S. 92 (1972).
32. *Ibid.* at 96. *See also Perry v. Perry,* 460 U.S. 37, 44 (1983) (a public forum exists from tradition or where the government intends to designate a place not traditionally open to debate as a public forum and the state must show any content-based regulation is necessary to serve a compelling state interest and be narrowly drawn to achieve that end); *Cornelius v. NAACP,* 105 S. Ct. 3439 (1985) (a limited public forum exists where the state designates a place not traditionally open to debate for a particular purpose, for example, where a public school is opened to persons/groups for activities related to school activity). *Note also Pickering v. Board of Education,* 391 U.S. 563 (1968) (even if no public forum exists, persons legitimately on the premises cannot be restricted in their speech on the basis of

content unless such would cause a substantial disruption or impede performance). ˙

33. *Ibid.* at 99-100.
34. *See e.g., Danskin v. San Diego Unified School District,* 28 Cal. 2d 536, 171 P. 2d 885 (1946).
35. 393 U.S. at 512, 513. While *Tinker* did not specifically consider the public forum doctrine, some legal scholars believe that the *Tinker* decision had the effect of establishing a public forum in the public schools. *See e.g.,* Garrison, *The Public School as Public Forum,* 54 Texas Law Review 90 (1975); Horning, *The First Amendment Right to a Public Forum,* 1969 Duke Law Journal 931, 944.
36. *See e.g., Country Hills Christian Church v. Unified School District No. 512,* 560 F. Supp. 1207 (D. Kan. 1983); *Garvin v. Rosenau,* 455 F.2d 233 (6th Cir. 1972); *Bender v. Williamsport Area School District,* 106 S. Ct. 1326 (1986); *Wilson v. Chancellor,* 418 F. Supp. 1358 (D. Or. 1976); *Lawrence University Bicentennial Commission v. City of Appleton,* 409 F. Supp. 1319 (E.D. Wis. 1976); *Vail v. Board of Education,* 354 F. Supp. 592 (D. N.H. 1973); *See also Planned Parenthood Association / Chicago Area v. Chicago Transit Authority,* 592 F. Supp. 544 (N.D. Ill. 1984); *United States v. Albertini,* 710 F. 2d 1410 (9th Cir. 1983). *But cf. Student Coalition for Peace v. Lower Merion School District,* 596 F. Supp. 169 (E.D. Pa. 1984).
37. 409 F. Supp. 1319 (E.D. Wis. 1976).
38. *Ibid.* at 1322-24.
39. 354 F. Supp. 592 (D. N.H. 1973), *vacated,* 502 F. 2d 1159 (1st Cir. 1973).
40. *Ibid.* at 601.
41. 454 U.S. 263 (1981).
42. *Ibid.* at 267, 268. Some confusion yet exists as to how far the public forum concept should be extended. One federal court of appeals, for example, has said: "While students have First Amendment rights to political speech in public schools . . . sensitive Establishment Clause considerations limit their right to air religious doctrines." *Lubbock Civil Liberties Union v. Lubbock Independent School District,* 669 F.2d 1038, 1048 (5th Cir. 1982), cert. denied, 459 U.S. 115 (1983), quoting from *Brandon v. Board of Education of Guilderland Central School District,* 635 F. 2d, 771, 980 (2d Cir. 1980). This statement runs contrary to a large body of decisions which hold that content-related regulation of speech is unconstitutional. *See also Bender v. Williamsport Area School District,* 106 S. Ct. 1326 (1986). *Cf.*

Chapman v. Thomas, 743 F.2d 1056 (4th Cir. 1984), *cert. grant-ed,* 53 U.S.L.W. 3700 (1985).

43. Comment, *Developments in the Law—Academic Freedom,* 81 Harvard Law Review 1045, 1134 (1968). *See Country Hills Christian Church v. Unified School District No. 512,* 560 F. Supp. 1207 (D. Kan. 1983), where it was held that by allowing school facilities to be used during nonschool hours by nonschool community groups, public school authorities created a public forum for exercise of First Amendment rights.

44. The Fourteenth Amendment equal protection clause reads: "No State shall . . . deny to any person within its jurisdiction the equal protection of the laws."

45. *See e.g., Snyder v. Board of Trustees,* 286 F. Supp. 927 (N.D. Ill. S.D. 1968); *Brooks v. Auburn University,* 296 F. Supp. 188 (M.D. Ala. E.D. 1969), *aff'd,* 412 F.2d 1171 (5th Cir. 1969); and, *Stacy v. Williams,* 306 F. Supp. 963 (N.D. Miss. W.D. 1969).

46. *Ibid.*

47. 306 F. Supp. 963 (N.D. Miss. W.D. 1969), *aff'd,* 446 F.2d 1366 (5th Cir. 1971).

48. *Ibid.* at 975-76.

49. *Ibid.* at 974.

50. *Frasca v. Andrews,* 463 F. Supp. 1043, 1050 (E.D. N.Y. 1979).

51. *See e.g., Shanley v. Northeast Independent School District, Bexar County, Texas,* 462 F. 2d 960 (5th Cir. 1972).

52. 453 F. 2d 54 (4th Cir. 1971). *Cf. Kania v. Fordham,* 702 F. 2d 475 (4th Cir. 1983).

53. *Ibid.* at 58 (emphasis supplied). *See also Baughman v. Freienmuth,* 478 F. 2d 1345 (4th Cir. 1973).

54. *See generally Grove v. Mead School District,* 753 F. 2d 1528 (9th Cir. 1985), *cert. denied,* 54 U.S.L.W. 3224 (Oct. 7, 1985).

55. *Ibid.*

56. 425 F. 2d 10 (7th Cir. 1970), *cert. denied,* 400 U.S. 826 (1970).

57. *Ibid.* at 13 n.5.

58. *Brooks v. Auburn University,* 296 F. Supp. 188, 196 (M.D. Ala. E.D.), *aff'd,* 412 F. 2d 1171 (5th Cir. 1969).

Chapter Four

1. *Police Department of Chicago v. Mosley,* 408 U.S. 92, 95 (1972).

2. *Red Lion Broadcasting Company v. Federal Communications Commission,* 395 U.S. 367, 390 (1969).

3. *Poe v. Ullman,* 367 U.S. 497, 514 (1961) (Douglas, J., dissenting) (emphasis supplied).

4. *Shelton v. Tucker,* 364 U.S. 479, 487 (1960). *See also Kingsley*

International Picture Corporation v. Regents of University of State of New York, 360 U.S. 684, 688 (1959), where the Supreme Court stated that the "First Amendment's basic guarantee is of freedom to advocate ideas."

5. *See e.g., Thornhill v. Alabama,* 310 U.S. 88, 95 (1940).

6. *Keyishian v. Board of Regents,* 385 U.S. 589, 603 (1967).

7. *Ibid.*

8. *Epperson v. Arkansas,* 393 U.S. 97, 114 (Black, J. concurring) (1968).

9. *See in general Albaum v. Carey,* 283 F. Supp. 3 (E.D. N.Y. 1968) (the state may not deny tenure or job benefits because of the teacher's exercise of free speech). *See also Dombrowski v. Pfister,* 380 U.S. 479, 85 S. Ct. 1116, 14 L. Ed. 2d 22 (1965) (conversations about teacher organizations cannot be prohibited); *Hastings v. Bonner,* 578 F. 2d 136, 143 (5th Cir. 1978) (a teacher has the freedom to associate by bringing others with her to her contract negotiations).

10. *See e.g., Sweezy v. New Hampshire,* 354 U.S. 234 (1957); *East Hartford Education Association v. Board of Education of East Hartford,* 562 F. 2d 838, 843 (2d Cir. 1977).

11. *Epperson v. Arkansas,* 393 U.S. 97, 104-05 (1968). *See in general Birdwell v. Hazelwood School District,* 352 F. Supp. 613 (E.D. Mo. 1972), *aff'd,* 491 F.2d 490 (8th Cir. 1974); *Mailloux v. Kiley,* 323 F. Supp. 1387 (D. Mass. 1971), *aff'd,* 448 F. 2d 1242 (1st Cir. 1971); *Keefe v. Geanakos,* 418 F. 2d 359 (1st Cir. 1969); *Sterling v. Fort Bend Independent School District,* 376 F. Supp. 657, 661-62 (S.D. Tex. 1972), vacated on other grounds, 496 F. 2d 92 (5th Cir. 1974); *Moore v. Gaston County Board of Education,* 357 F. Supp. 1037 (W.D. N.C. 1973); *Parducci v. Rutland,* 316 F. Supp. 352 (M.D. Ala. 1970); *Lindros v. Governing Board of Torrance Unified School District,* 108 Cal. Rptr. 185, 510 P. 2d 361, *cert. denied,* 414 U.S. 1112 (1973); Nahmod, *Controversy in the Classroom: The High School Teacher and Freedom of Expression,* 39 George Washington Law Review 1032 (1972); Van Alstyne, *The Constitutional Rights of Teachers and Professors,* 1970 Duke Law Journal 841; Project, *Education and the Law: State Interests and Individual Rights,* 74 Michigan Law Review 1373 (1976); Note, *Academic Freedom in the Public Schools: The Right to Teach,* 48 New York University Law Review 1176 (1973).

12. 393 U.S. 503, 506 (1969). *See also Connecticut State Federation of Teachers v. Board of Education Members,* 538 F. 2d 471, 478 (2d Cir. 1976).

13. 461 F.2d 566 (2d Cir. 1972), *cert. denied,* 409 U.S. 1042 (1972), *reh'g denied,* 410 U.S. 947 (1973).

14. *Ibid.* at 571. The *Tinker* test states that free expression is guaranteed in the public schools unless it (1) materially and substantially interferes with the requirements of appropriate discipline in the operation of the school and (2) does not invade the rights of others. 393 U.S. at 513. *See Texas State Teachers Association v. Garland Independent School District,* 777 F.2d. 1046, 1053 (5th Cir. 1985) (teachers' communications may be suppressed only when they materially or substantially interfere with the activities or discipline of the school).
15. *Ibid.* at 572.
16. *Ibid.* at 573.
17. 393 U.S. at 511; *Burnside v. Byars,* 363 F. 2d 744, 749 (5th Cir. 1966).
18. *Giboney v. Empire Storage and Ice Company,* 336 U.S. 490, 501-02 (1949); *Cox v. Louisiana,* 379 U.S. 559, 564 (1965), *reh'g denied,* 380 U.S. 926 (1965).
19. 408 U.S. 169 (1972).
20. *Ibid.* at 187-88. *See National Gay Task Force v. Board of Education of the Oklahoma City,* 729 F.2d 1270 (10th Cir. 1984), *aff'd.* by an equally divided court, 53 U.S.L.W. 4408 (1985), where a statute which restricted the advocacy of homosexuality was, in part, held in violation of First Amendment right of free expression.
21. *Epperson v. Arkansas,* 393 U.S. 97, 107 (1968).
22. *Russo v. Central School District No. 1, Town of Rush v. County of Monroe, State of New York,* 469 F. 2d 623, 631-32 (2d Cir. 1972), *cert. denied,* 411 U.S. 932 (1973).
23. 461 F.2d 566 (2d Cir. 1972), *cert. denied,* 409 U.S. 1042 (1972), *reh'g denied,* 410 U.S. 987 (1973).
24. *See e.g., Epperson v. Arkansas,* 393 U.S. 97, 104 (1968).
25. 461 F. 2d at 573.
26. 418 F. Supp. 1358 (D. Or. 1976).
27. *Ibid.* at 1361-62.
28. *Ibid.* at 1363.
29. *Ibid.* at 1366, 1367.
30. *Ibid.* at 1363.
31. *Ibid.*
32. *Ibid.* at 1363, 1367.
33. *Ibid.* at 1364.
34. *Ibid.*
35. *See in general Amalgamated Food Employees Union Local 590 v. Logan Valley Plaza, Inc.,* 391 U.S. 308 (1968).
36. *See Breen v. Runkel,* 614 F. Supp. 355 (W.D. Mich.1985), where-

in it was held that a teacher's practice of leading prayers and Bible reading in the classroom constituted state action.

37. *Williams v. Eaton,* 443 F. 2d 422, 433 (10th Cir. 1971), *dismissed* 333 F. Supp. 107 (D. Wyo. 1971).
38. 461 F. 2d 566 (2d Cir. 1972).
39. *Ibid.* at 568.
40. *Keefe v. Geanokos,* 418 F. 2d 359, 362, n. 9 (1st Cir. 1969), *citing Wieman v. Updegraff,* 344 U.S. 183, 194, 195 (1952); and, *Mailloux v. Kiley,* 448 F. 2d 1242, 1243 (1st Cir. 1971).
41. *Keyishian v. Board of Regents,* 385 U.S. 589, 604 (1967).
42. *Pred v. Board of Instruction of Dade County, Florida,* 415 F. 2d 851, 857, n. 17 (5th Cir. 1969).

Chapter Five

1. *See, in general, International Society for Krishna Consciousness, Inc. v. Rockford,* 425 F. Supp. 734 (N.D. Ill. 1977) *(modified on app.* 585 F. 2d 263) (7th Cir. 1978); *Krishna v. Hays,* 438 F. Supp. 1077 (S.D. Fla. 1977); *Krishna v. Griffin,* 437 F. Supp. 666 (W.D. Pa. 1977); *Krishna v. Bowen,* 456 F. Supp. 437 (S.D. Ind. 1978), *aff'd,* 600 F. 2d 667 (7th Cir. 1979), *cert. denied,* 444 U.S. 963 (1979); *Krishna v. McAvey,* 450 F. Supp. 1265 (S.D. N.Y. 1978); *Krishna v. Lentini,* 461 F. Supp. 49 (E.D. La. 1978); *Krishna v. Kearnes,* 454 F. Supp. 116 (E.D. Cal. 1978); *Liberman v. Schesventer,* 447 F. Supp. 1355 (M.D. Fla. 1978); *United States v. Boesewetter,* 463 F. Supp. 370 (D.C. D.C. 1978); *Holy Spirit Association for the Unification of World Christianity v. Alley,* 460 F. Supp. 346 (N.D. Tex. 1978); *Fernandes v. Limmer,* 465 F. Supp. 493 (N.D. Tex. 1979), *modified* 663 F. 2d 619 (5th Cir. 1981), *cert. dismissed,* 103 S. Ct. 5 (1982); *United States v. Silberman,* 464 F. Supp. 866 (M.D. Fla. 1979).
2. *See in general West Virginia State Board of Education v. Barnette,* 319 U.S. 624, 639 (1943). For a more recent case *see May v. Evansville-Vanderburgh School Corp.,* 787 F.2d 1105 (7th Cir. 1986), wherein an appellate court refused to create a new constitutional right which would allow public employees an absolute free speech right simply by virtue of the fact that they were public employees, especially, as in this case, when the employer did not permit meetings except for business purposes. However, the court indicated that had Mrs. May made a free exercise claim, rather than a free speech claim, especially under the rather unusual circumstances, the case may have been decided differently. *Ibid.* at 17.

3. *Thomas v. Collins,* 323 U.S. 516, 530 (1945).
4. *See e.g., Fernandes v. Limmer,* 465 F. Supp. 493 (N.D. Tex. 1979), modified 663 F. 2d 619 (5th Cir. 1981), *cert. dismissed,* 458 U.S. 1124 (1982), citing *Marsh v. Alabama,* 326 U.S. 501 (1946).
5. *See in general Buckley v. Valeo,* 424 U.S. 1, 48, 49 (1976).
6. *Lamont v. Postmaster General,* 381 U.S. 301, 309 (1965).
7. 454 U.S. 263 (1981).
8. *Ibid.* at 270, 271.
9. *Ibid.* at 271.
10. *Ibid.* at 273.
11. 408 U.S. 169 (1972).
12. *Ibid.* at 180 (citing *Shelton v. Tucker,* 364 U.S. 479, 487 (1960)).
13. 354 F. Supp. 592 (D. N.H. 1973), *vacated,* 502 F. 2d 1159 (2d Cir. 1973).
14. *Ibid.* at 601. *See also in general Garvin v. Rosenau,* 455 F.2d 233 (6th Cir. 1972); *Wilson v. Chancellor,* 418 F. Supp. 1348 (D. Or. 1976); *Lawrence University Bicentennial Commission v. City of Appleton,* 409 F. Supp. 1319 (E.D. Wis. 1976); *Vail v. Board of Education,* 354 F. Supp. 592 (D.N.H.), *vacated,* 502 F. 2d 1159 (1st Cir. 1973); *ACLU v. Radford College,* 315 F. Supp. 893 (W.D. Va. 1970); *Molpus v. Fortune,* 311 F. Supp. 240 (N.D. Miss. 1970); *Smith v. University of Tennessee,* 300 F. Supp. 777 (E.D. Tenn. 1969); *Brooks v. Auburn University,* 296 F. Supp. 188 (M.D. Ala. 1969); *Snyder v. Board of Education,* 286 F. Supp. 927 (N.D. Ill. 1968).
15. *See in general* Garrison, *The Public School as a Public Forum,* 54 Texas Law Review 90 (1975); Horning, *The First Amendment Right to a Public Forum,* 1969 Duke Law Journal 931; Nahmod, *Beyond Tinker: The High School as an Educational Public Forum,* 5 Harvard C.R.—C.L.L Review, 278 (1970). Garrison has concluded

    "[I]n some public places the first amendment must have substantive safeguards—i.e., in the traditional forum where everyone may communicate in widely varying ways, and in certain other places where a more limited group of speakers may express themselves in more limited modes. *Tinker. . .* speaks to the latter situation and recognizes that individuals carry first amendment rights wherever they have a right to go."
    Garrison at 111.
16. *See in general Stacy v. Williams,* 306 F. Supp. 963 (N.D. Miss. 1969), aff'd., 446 F. 2d 1366 (5th Cir. 1971); *Riseman v. School Committee of City of Quincy,* 439 F. 2d 148 (1st Cir. 1971); *cf.*

Lehman v. City of Shaker Heights, 418 U.S. 298, 311 (1974), where Justice Brennan in his dissenting opinion, *citing Cox v. Louisiana,* 379 U.S. 536, 554 (1965), stated: " 'The rights of free speech and assembly . . . still do not mean that everyone with opinions or beliefs to express may address a group at any public place and at any time.' " He further stated, "We have repeatedly recognized the constitutionality of reasonable 'time, place and manner' regulations which are applied in an even-handed fashion." (dissenting opinions by Brennan, Stewart, Marshall, Powell, J.J.) *(citing Police Department of Chicago v. Mosley,* 408 U.S. 92, 98 (1972)); *see also Grayned v. City of Rockford,* 408 U.S. 104, 115 (1972); *Cox v. Louisiana,* 379 U.S. 536, 554-55 (1965); *Poulos v. New Hampshire,* 345 U.S. 395, 398 (1953); *Cox v. New Hampshire,* 312 U.S. 569, 575-76 (1941); *Schneider v. State,* 308 U.S. 147, 160 (1939); *Amalgamated Food Employees Union v. Logan Valley Plaza, Inc.,* 391 U.S. 308, 320 (1968).

17. 409 F. Supp. 1319 (E.D. Wis. 1976).
18. 560 F. Supp. 1207 (D. Kan. 1983).
19. *Ibid.* at 1322-24; 560 F. Supp. at 1215.
20. 306 F. Supp. 963 (N.D. Miss. 1969).
21. *Ibid.* at 975, n. 28.
22. *Ibid.* at 975-76.
23. *Bantam Books, Inc. v. Sullivan,* 372 U.S. 58, 70 (1963); *Near v. Minnesota,* 283 U.S. 697, 715-716 (1931); *Lovell v. Griffin,* 303 U.S. 444, 451, 452 (1938); *Schneider v. State,* 308 U.S. 147, 164 (1939); *Cantwell v. Connecticut,* 310 U.S. 296, 306 (1940); *Neimotko v. Maryland,* 340 U.S. 268, 273 (1951); *Kunz v. New York,* 340 U.S. 290, 293 (1951); *Staub v. Baxley,* 355 U.S. 313, 321 (1958); *Freedman v. Maryland,* 380 U.S. 51, 57 (1965); *Carroll v. Princess Anne,* 393 U.S. 175, 181 (1968); *Nebraska Press Association v. Stuart, Judge, et al.,* 427 U.S. 539, 559 (1976).

Chapter Six

1. Congressional Record, Senate (June 6, 1984), § 6651.
2. *Ibid.,* (June 27, 1984), § 8331.
3. *Ibid.,* § 8337.
4. Since its enactment the courts have construed the Equal Access Act in a number of cases. *See e.g., Amidei v. Spring Branch Independent School District,* No. H-84-4673 (S.D. Tex. May 9, 1985); *Student Coalition for Peace v. Lower Merion School District Board of School Directors,* 776 F. 2d 437 (3rd Cir. 1985); *Salinas*

v. School District of Kansas City, Missouri, 751 F. 2d 288 (8th Cir. 1984); *Mergens v. Board of Education,* No. 85-0-426 (D. Neb. Complaint filed April 17, 1985) *as cited* in The National Law Journal, June 24, 1985 at 16, col. 3; and, *Bell v. Little Axe Independent School District No. 70,* 766 F. 2d 1391 (10th Cir. 1985).

5. 106 S. Ct. 1326 (1986).
6. *Equal Access: First Amendment Question,* Hearing before the Senate Committee on the Judiciary, 98th Cong., 2nd Sess. (April 28, 1983), p. 45.
7. *Ibid.,* p. 82.
8. *Ibid.,* p. 37.
9. *Ibid.,* pp. 56-57.
10. *Ibid.,* p. 38.
11. *Ibid.,* p. 66.
12. *See Action by Attorney General,* S. 1059, § 4(a) (1).
13. 454 U.S. 263 (1981).
14. 130 Cong. Rec. § 8342 (June 12, 1984).
15. 393 U.S. 503 (1969).
16. *Ibid.,* at 513.

Chapter Seven

1. 323 U.S. 516 (1945).
2. *Ibid.* at 543.
3. *Ibid.* at 530.
4. 308 U.S. 147 (1939).
5. *Ibid.* at 163.
6. 408 U.S. 169 (1972).
7. *Ibid.* at 183.

About the Author

John W. Whitehead, an attorney specializing in constitutional law, is president of the Rutherford Institute, headquartered in Manassas, Virginia. He has successfully litigated many constitutional law cases.

Mr. Whitehead has taught constitutional law and courses on the First Amendment. He has also lectured at various law schools throughout the United States.

He has served as counsel to numerous organizations. He has also served as counsel *amicus curiae* in the United States Supreme Court and various United States Circuit Courts.

Mr. Whitehead is a member of the bars of the Supreme Courts of Virginia and Arkansas; the United States Supreme Court; the United States Courts of Appeals for the Fourth, Seventh, and Ninth Circuits; and various United States District Courts. He has also been appointed Special Assistant Attorney General for the State of Louisiana.

Mr. Whitehead has authored ten books and has coauthored others. The film version of his book *The Second American Revolution* has been made by Franky

Schaeffer V Productions of Los Gatos, California. The movie has been screened in the White House and before congressional staffs in Washington, D.C. It was nationally premiered in November 1982 at the National Archives in Washington, D.C.

Mr. Whitehead has also published articles in both *Emory Law Journal* and *Texas Tech Law Review.* Both concerned First Amendment issues.

He is married and the father of five children.

The Rutherford Institute

The Rutherford Institute is a Virginia-based legal and educational organization that defends religious persons whose constitutional rights have been threatened by state action.

The Institute has assisted both teachers and students denied the freedom of expression in the public schools.

For example, the Institute successfully defended a Florida sixth-grader after school officials confiscated the New Testaments that she had handed out to classmates after her book report on the Bible. That action, followed by school officials' interrogation and harassment of the student, sparked a lawsuit against the school district for violating her First Amendment rights. The Institute attained a court order that protected the student's right to exercise her freedom of speech at school.

In a case in Minnesota, the Institute filed suit on behalf of two high school students who were suspended for passing out copies of a religious newspaper in the school hallways. Although the case was declared moot after the students graduated, the school district dropped its policy of prohibiting the distribution of religious literature on school property.

In Montclair, California, Institute attorneys gained another victory when the school board agreed that a high school junior had the constitutional right to pass out pamphlets on school property. As another concession, the school district agreed to set up orientation workshops to educate teachers and administrators on students' rights to free speech.

In Indiana the Institute defended a public school teacher's aide who sued the school district after she and some colleagues were forbidden to meet on campus in the morning for Bible study and prayer. A court of appeals ruled the meetings unconstitutional, although teachers in the school *are* allowed to meet and discuss all other topics of interest.

In addition to defending the freedom of religious expression in the public schools, Institute attorneys also participate in legal action to protect other vital constitutional rights. To make its services more accessible, the Institute has begun building a network of state chapters, with the goal of having at least one chapter in all fifty states.

To educate the public on priority issues, the Institute publishes numerous books and papers and holds seminars around the country. Its legal briefs are also available to other attorneys involved in similar litigation.

Address: The Rutherford Institute, P.O. Box 510, Manassas, VA 22110.